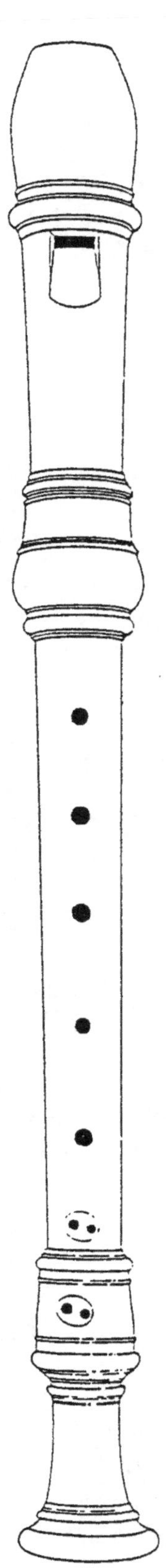

# *The Charlton Method for the Recorder*

## *A Manual for the Advanced Recorder Player*

*Second Edition*

Andrew Charlton

Peacock Press
Scout Bottom Farm
Mytholmroyd
Hebden Bridge
West Yorkshire
HX7 5JS (UK)

*To Kathie, without whose concern for my well-being this book would have been finished several months sooner.*

*Peacock Press*
*Scout Bottom Farm, Mytholmroyd*
*Hebden Bridge, West Yorkshire, HX7 5JS (UK)*

*First published 1981 by The Curators of the University of Missouri*
*Reprinted 2015 by Peacock Press*

*ISBN 978-1-908904-79-9*

*Front cover image by Helen Hooker*

*Printed in Great Britain by*
*Lightning Source. UK*

# Contents

# *Preface*

This manual grew out of materials that the author had developed over many years of teaching university courses in Interpretation of Early Music, Collegium Musicum, Renaissance Ensemble, and Baroque Ensemble as well as applied instruction in recorder and other "early" instruments. This method should be used by the adult student (or serious younger student), one with some background in music who is studying with an instructor, either individually or in a class, or one whose musical training has been extensive enough that he/she can carry on a program self-study without falling into the sorts of bad habits all too common with the self-taught. There are no introductory charts of note types or lists of musical terms usually associated with beginning methods as it is assumed that most of these musical fundamentals have long since become part of the student's vocabulary or, lacking this background, that there is a teacher guiding him/her who will present these materials as they are needed.

In order for this manual to be utilized in the manner in which it is conceived, the student must work on at least two members of the recorder family, one in C and one if F, from the very first lesson. It is suggested that these be soprano and alto, or possibly soprano and sopranino, or some such combination of the two notational types.

The Modern Recorder Family Consists Of:

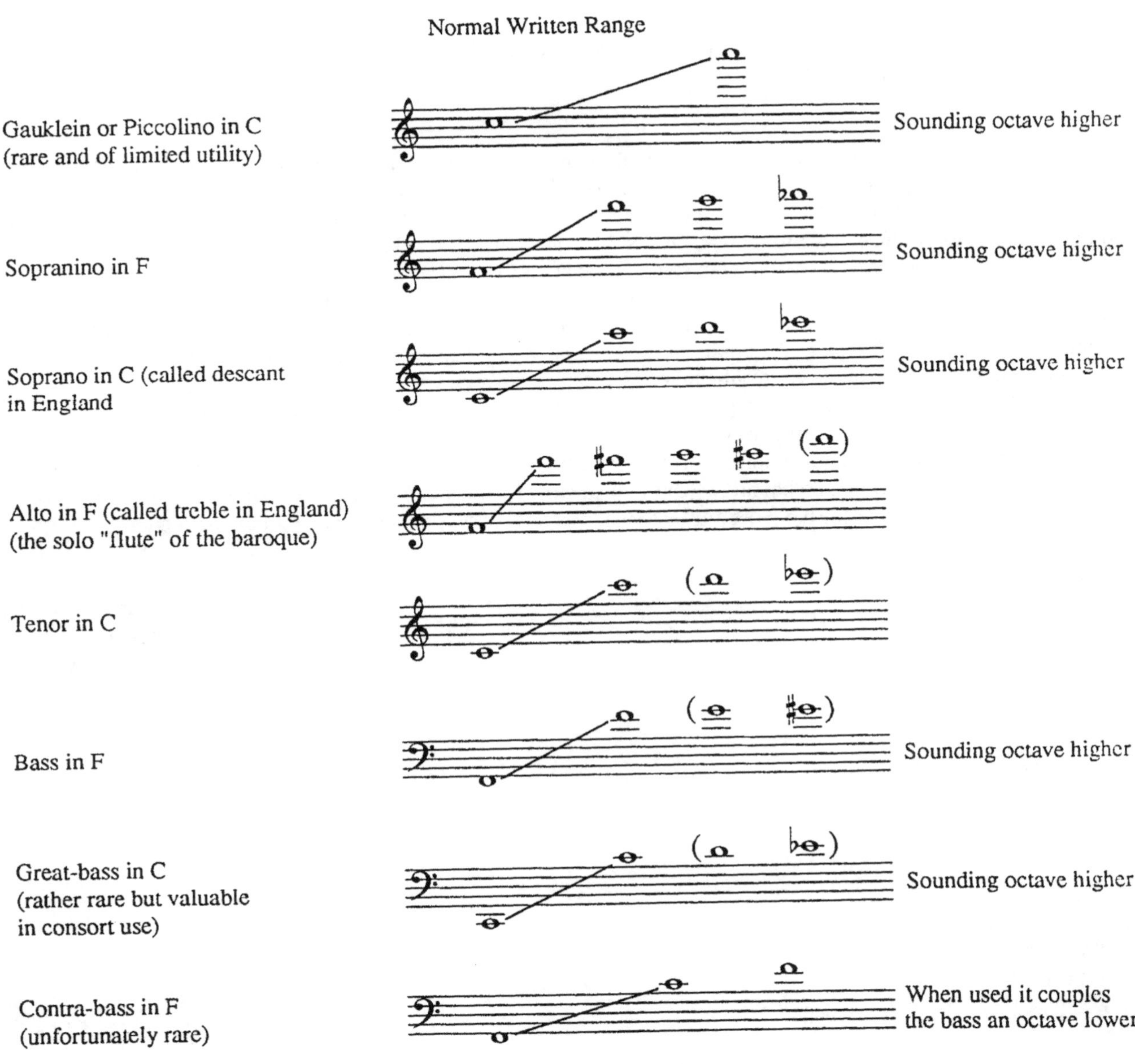

The above chart shows the usual method of notating the members of the recorder family; however, certain instruments are often called on to read in octaves other than those indicated. For instance, the alto is often written an octave lower than it sounds so that the player is obliged to transpose up an octave. Occasionally the bass is written at actual sounding pitch in the treble clef so the player must make the necessary adjustment in order that the correct octave relationships with other parts be maintained. When playing music written for recorders be aware of the small number eight over (or rarely under) the clef sign as this indicates the actual sounding pitch of the music.

The range chart on the previous page applies mainly to instruments with a baroque bore, that is, a reverse cone of rather small dimensions. The renaissance bore is generally cylindrical with larger dimensions making for an instrument with more power, especially in the lower register, but with a more limited upper register. Usually the renaissance instruments lack the top third or even fourth of the baroque instruments. It is not wise to use both types in the same consort as the larger-bore renaissance will overpower the softer baroque instruments.

Fingering for specific notes will be indicated by the following type of diagram. The circles represent holes in the body of the instrument which when blackened indicate that the corresponding hole is to covered. The diagram will be presented either vertically or horizontally so that the left hand will either be on the top or to the left.

| | | | |
|---|---|---|---|
| Thumb | OO | First Finger | |
| | O | Second Finger | Left Hand |
| | O | Third Finger | |
| | ——— | | |
| | O | First Finger | |
| | O | Second Finger | Right Hand |
| | oo | Third Finger | |
| | oo | Fourth Finger | |

Some instruments may lack either or both of the sets of double holes at the bottom, or there may be single or double keys instead of holes. If there are only single holes for the last two fingers, it means that two of the low accidentals will be very difficult or even impossible to produce. On some instruments half covering the bottom holes will give rather fuzzy tones that will require some skill to make them sound musical and in tune.

You will notice that starting with some of the notes in the second register the left thumb has the indication to half cover the hole. Your teacher will show the correct hand and thumb position for this. Acoustically this changes the pressure requirements for the standing wave in the bore causing it to split into two parts producing the octave. The optimum size of the small leak in the thumb hole will vary from instrument to instrument so some experimentation will show what will produce to best results in terms of tone quality and intonation.

Starting with exercises on page one it is important that you practice an equal amount of time on each recorder. Do not allow one fingering, or rather notational, system to become dominant in your mind.

Initially, be sure that you tongue each note with a soft "tah" or whatever syllable your teacher prefers; sustain each note for its value; do not allow your tone to wobble (more about vibrato later); and, above all, be critical of your own sound, striving for the most musical results and not accepting anything less than perfection.

Happy Playing—

Andrew Charlton
Anaheim, California
January 1981

When there is more than one fingering for a particular note, the first fingering is usually the preferred or regular one. All other fingerings are to be considered alternates. Not all fingerings are possible or in tune on all makes of recorders so you will have to experiment to find what works best on your instrument.

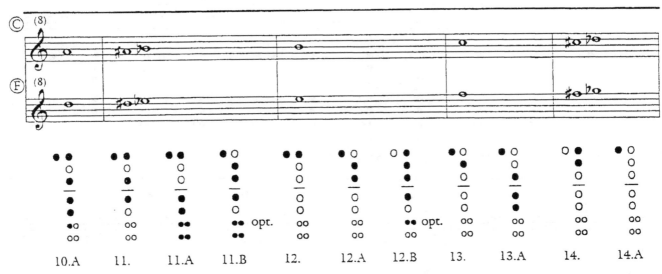

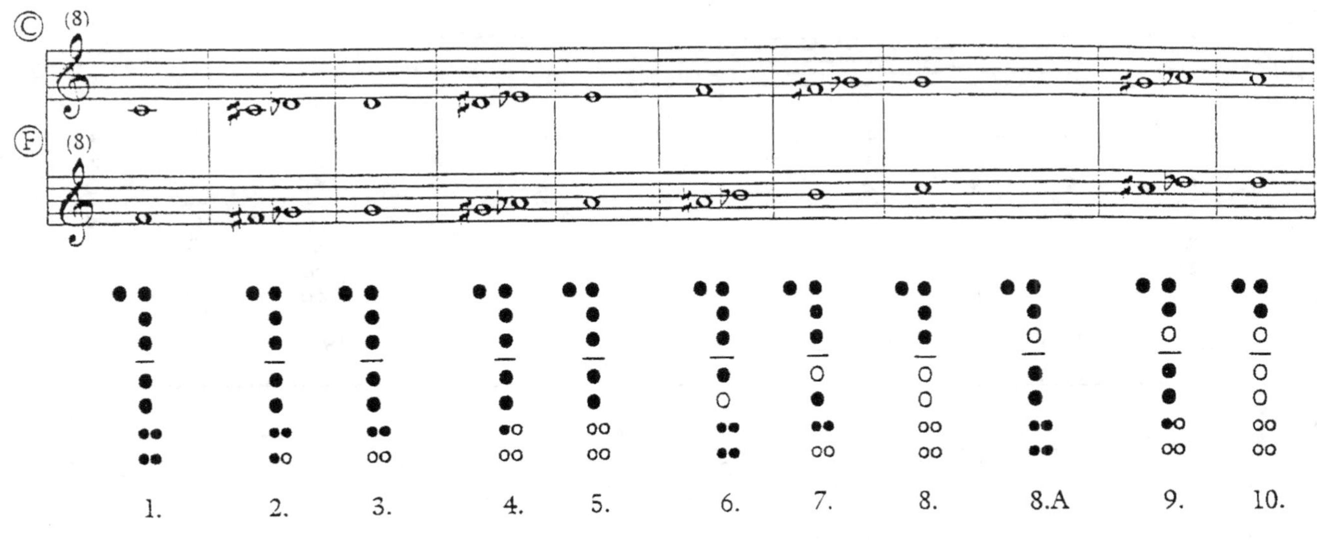


C (8)
F (8)

opt. opt.

10.A 11. 11.A 11.B 12. 12.A 12.B 13. 13.A 14. 14.A

C (8)
F (8)

opt.

14.B 15. 15.A 15.B 16. 16.A 16.B 16.C 17. 17.A 17.B

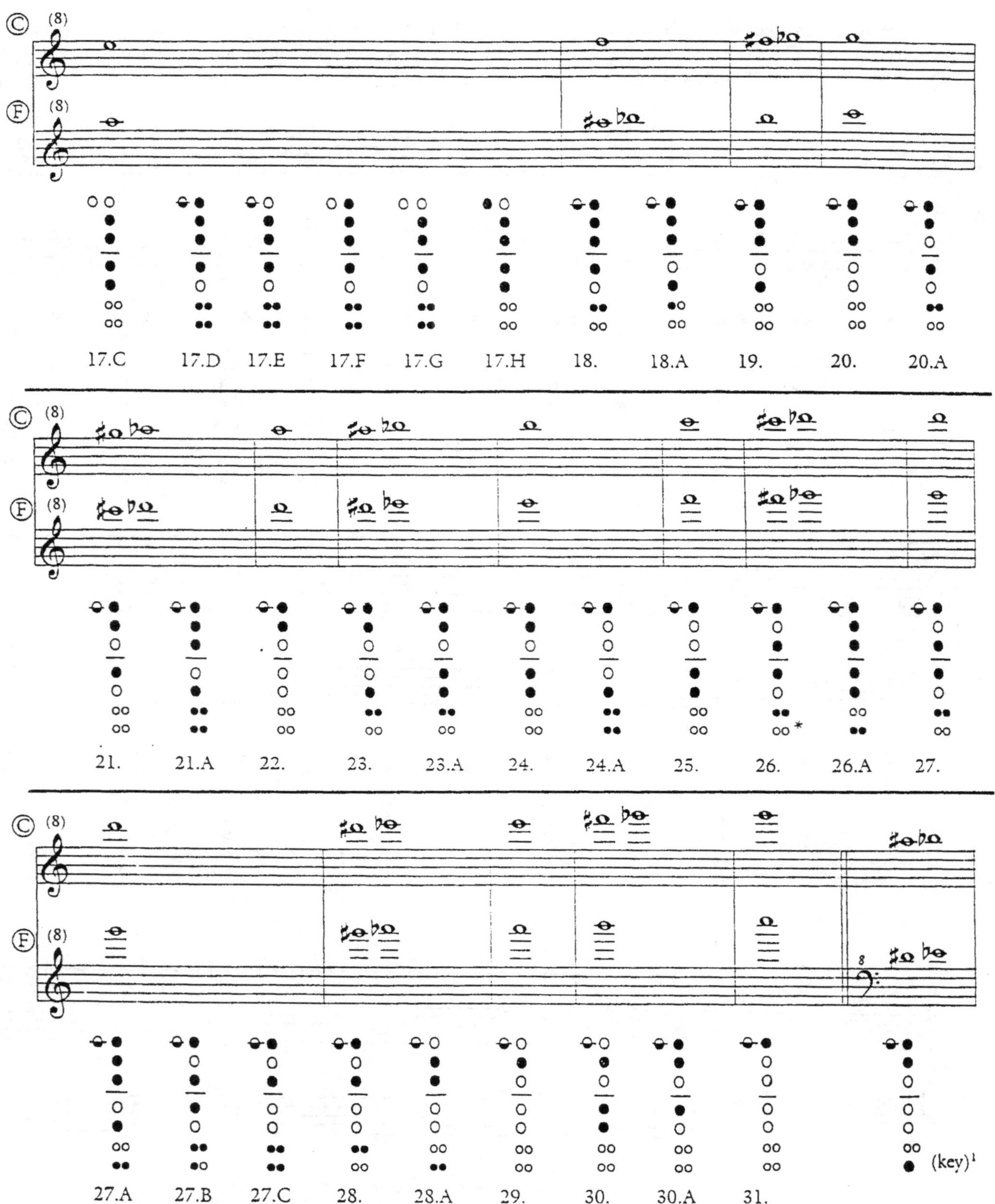


*This note requires either a bell key or stopping the end of the recorder with the knee.

1. This note on some tenors and basses requires this special fingering.

## *Trill Fingering Chart*



As most trills in early music start with the upper neighboring tone and trill down to the principal note, some of the following combinations will show one fingering for the initial note and another fingering for the same note after the trill starts. There are some trills that are not possible or highly impractical on the recorder so some gaps will appear in this chart.

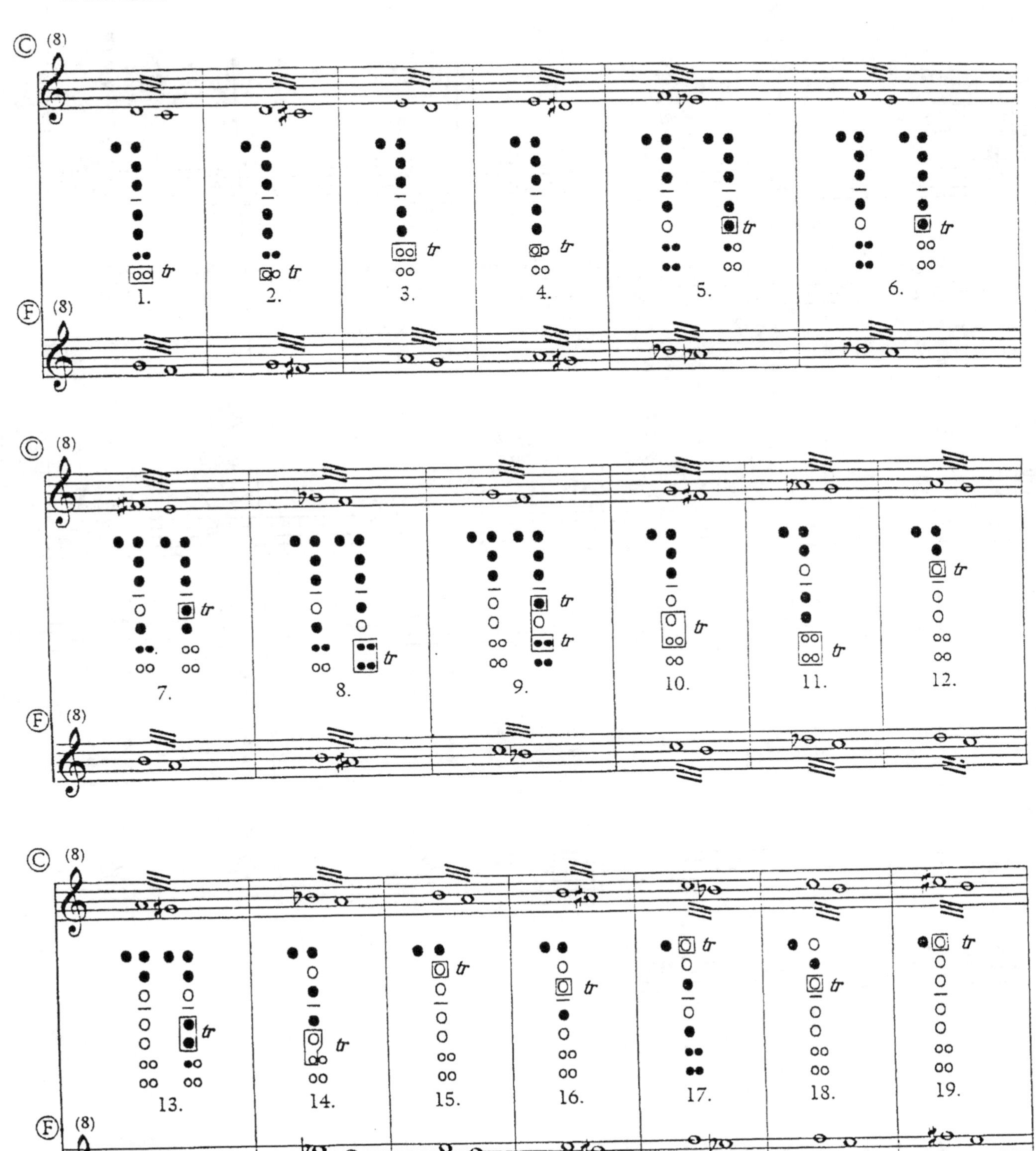

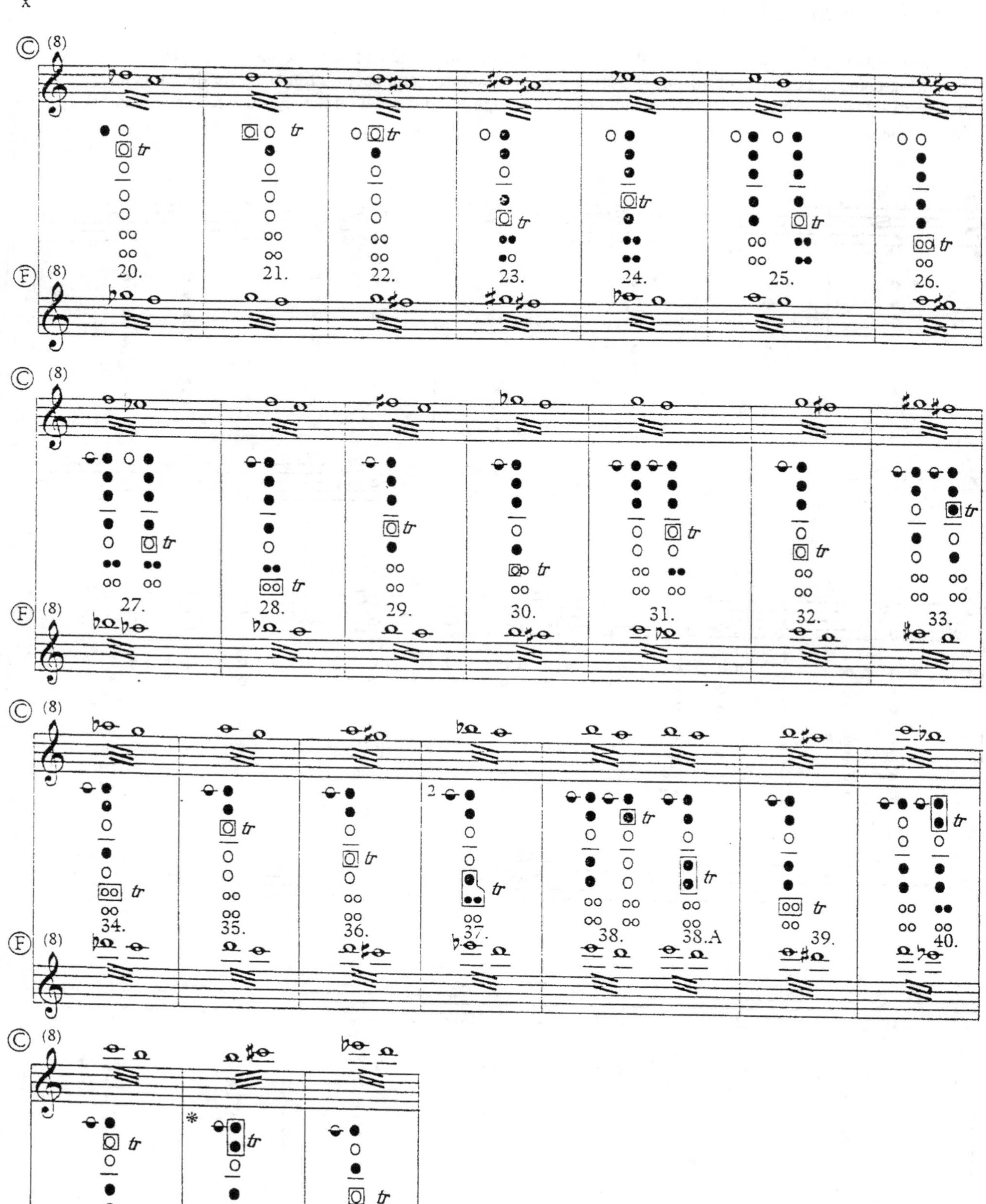


*The upper neighboring tone cannot be articulated.
2. On some tenors and basses, this trill can only be produced like this: K tr

# Basic Technique Exercises

Watch out for fingering combinations that require exchanging one finger for another. The B-C and D-B combinations on C recorders and the F-E and E-G combinations on F recorders are awkward and require much practice to make them smooth and musical.

Be sure to practice both parts on all duos. Do not allow one one notational system to become dominant in your mind. Use alto recorder on the second part, not sopranino as this would invert the parts resulting in incorrect voicing.

(8)
8.
9.

If the lowest one or two notes do not seem to speak clearly or at all or if they seem to want to go up the octave, one of two things may be wrong. Either the fingers are not completely and firmly closing all of the holes or too much air is being put into the instrument. On most recorders the lowest notes must be produced by blowing very lightly.

By now you will have encountered some problems of finger coordination involving the following note combinations:

The answer to these problems is, of course, to work out each of the problem combinations, developing the necessary motor coordination to the point that the notes can be played smoothly and effortlessly.

Ⓒ (8) 10.A

(8) B

(8) C

(8) D

(8) E

Ⓕ (8) 11.A

(8) B

(8) C

(8) D

(8) E

(8) F

(C) (8)
12.

(8)

(8)

(F) (8)
13.

(8)

(8)

(C) (8)
14.

(8)

(8)

(F) (8)
15.

(8)

(8)

The following is a canon for soprano and alto recorders. The soprano will start, playing all of the B's natural; the alto will start at the beginning when the soprano reaches the asterix (*) playing all of the B's flatted.

(8)
16. *

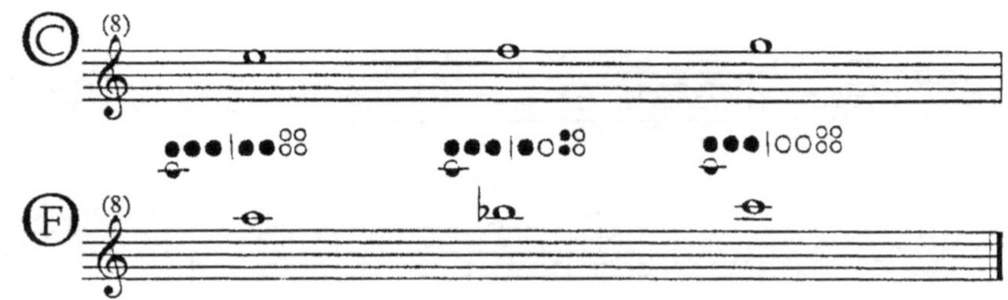


The half-hole thumb sign (◒) indicates that the left-hand thumb is to be bent at the joint, pushing the thumbnail into the hole producing an air leak the size of which can be adjusted by a slight motion of the thumb. Some adjusting of the size of the opening may be necessary as one ascends into the upper register in order to make certain notes "speak" clearly and to keep them in tune.

C (8)

17.

(8)

(8)

F (8)

18.

(8)

(8)

C (8)

19.

(8)

(8)

(8)

(8)

CANON AT THE OCTAVE The alto recorder enters at the beginning when the soprano reaches the asterisk.

♩. = 58 - 60

S
24
A

♩ 68 - 72

S
25
A

CANON AT THE FIFTH - The soprano recorder will start first at the beginning playing in the key of C; when the soprano gets to the asterisk, the alto will start at the beginning ***using C-recorder fingerings*** in the key of F:

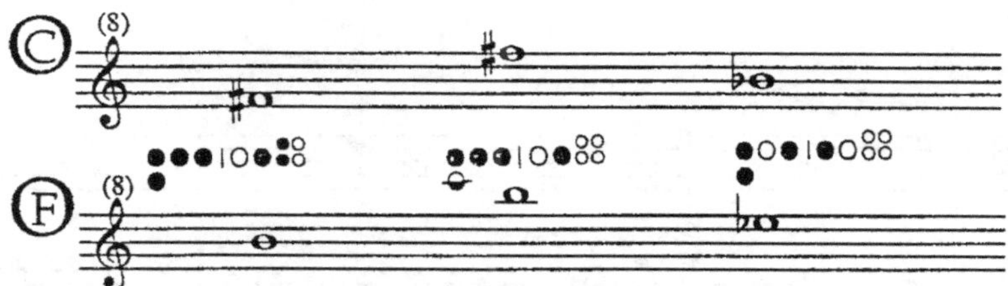

Because of differences among various makes of recorders, the third of these notes may have to be fingered either either 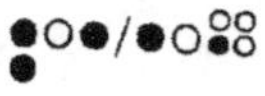 or 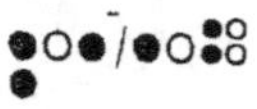 in order to be better in tune. Find which of these works best for you.

27.

28.

CANON AT THE OCTAVE - The soprano starts first and the alto starts when the soprano arrives at the asterisk.

C
(8)
34.
F
35.
rit.

Many fingering charts give  ●●○|●●○○ as the fingering for the second note, but on most makes of recorders this is too sharp; therefore, even though some passages may become a little awkward with the given fingering, use the additional hole.

Ⓒ (8) 36.

Ⓕ (8) 37.

Ⓒ (8) 38.

(8)

Ⓕ (8) 39.

(8)

Ⓒ (8) 40.

(8)

Ⓕ (8) 41.

(8)

Ⓒ (8) 42.

(8)

Ⓕ (8) 43.

(8)

CANON AT THE OCTAVE - The alto starts first; the soprano starts at the beginning when the alto gets to the asterisk.

At this point you have learned the basic fingerings for a chromatic octave and a sixth, with the exception of two accidentals in the lowest register. These two notes involve the use of the double holes for the right hand, or on some makes of instruments, keys are provided for one or both of them.

C
(8)
51.
F
52.

C
(8)
F
(8)
C
(8)
53.
3
4
(8)
F
(8)
54.
(8)
C
(8)
55.
(8)
F
(8)
56.
6
8
(8)
C
(8)
57.
3
(8)
3
3
3
3
F
(8)
58.
(8)

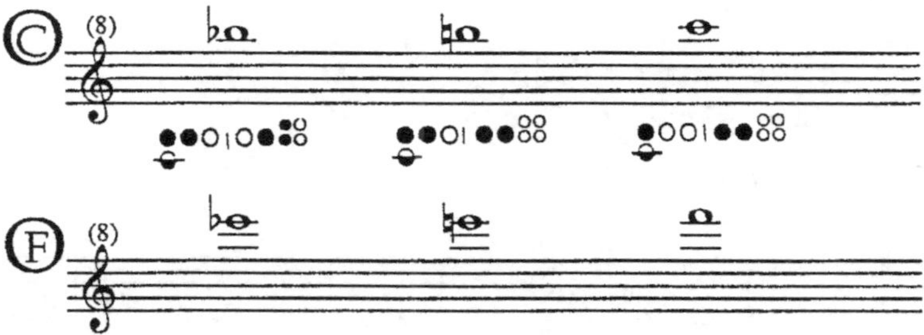


There may be a problem with the upper B-flat on some C recorders so try the following if the given fingering is not in tune:

On some makes of tenor recorder the low C key might have to be used: *Key*

C 59.

F 60.

C 61.

F 62.

C 63.

F 64.

# 65. Articulation Studies

Apply the articulation patterns (1 through 8) to the following exercises (A through T). Play each repeated bar four times. The exercises can also be used as finger coordination studies by ignoring the articulation patterns.

(8)
G.
H.
I.
J.
K.
L.
M.

(8)
N.
O.
P.
Q.
R.
S.
T.

# 66. Coordination Studies

These exercises are planned to help coordinate your fingers and tongue as well as to increase your ability to read nonrepetitive patterns quickly. Do not slight them but spend time in serious study of them.

©
67.
(8)
(8)
(8)
(8)
(8)
(8)
(8)
(8)
(8)
(8)
(8)
(8)
(8)
(8)

F
68.
(8)

# Interval Studies

A. THIRDS

C
71.
(8)
F
72.

B. FOURTHS

C. FIFTHS

D. SIXTHS

## E. SEVENTHS

F. OCTAVES

To this point we have explored the two-octave range of the recorder and have developed some facility within this compass. There are a few notes possible above this range, the fingering and practicability of which will vary from instrument to instrument. Most tenor and bass recorders cannot be pushed above the two-octave point comfortably as the quality is not usually very good even if the notes will speak.
The easiest of these higher notes to produce (although you will have to discover which fingering is best for your instrument) is:

It does not exist as a satisfactory usable note on most instruments although J.S. Bach wrote several high F-sharps for the first alto recorder in his Brandenburg Concerto No. 4. Some modern instrument makers will furnish a bell key on special order for both alto and soprano recorders so that this note becomes easy to produce, but, of course, this did not exist in Bach's time. Some fingering charts give as the fingering for this note, but it tends to be much too sharp on all makes of instrument. Some instruments can produce a reasonably in-tune note fingered . Instruments that can produce the high D-G using the first fingering (above) can then stop the end of the bell with the knee and get a good C-sharp, F-sharp. This is what the bell key accomplishes without the danger of having the player's bridgework dislocated.

One solution to the high F-sharp problem in the fourth Brandenburg involves a fingering that can only be approached by slurring from a half or whole step below. This technique requires a bit of skill to make it work. It calls for slurring to the F-sharp while giving a little push to the airstream. The F-sharp cannot be sustained but must be released at once:

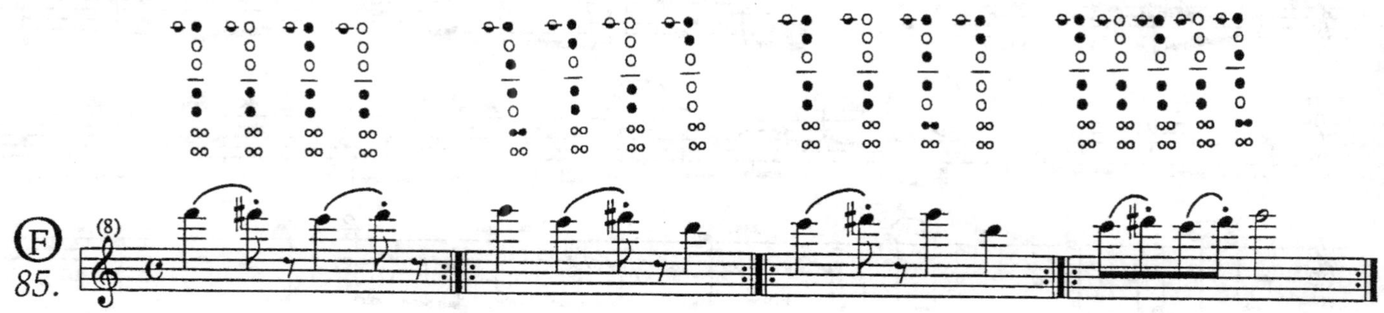

Following are two sections from the fourth Brandenburg showing where the E to F-sharp slurring technique may be used.

First Movement, Measures 47-53:

Third Movement, Measures 55-60

The slurs in the above examples are not Bach's, but show where the "trick" fingering can be used. Try the above passages using plus stopping the end of the recorder with the knee for the high F-sharp and you will see what the problem involved in playing this note can be. Obviously this fingering can only work if the player is sitting.

Most fingering charts only go up to the high D-G but there are a number of additional higher pitches that can be produced on most makes of recorders. One that is relatively to produce is the high E-flat, A-flat. Starting with the usual fingering for high D-G, it involves raising the right-hand first finger to produce the higher pitch:

There are other altissimo notes possible on the recorder but the quality is often less than desirable on most instruments—except those equipped with a bell key. There is one of these notes that you should be familiar with, however, as G. P. Telemann used it in one of his sonatas for alto recorder. This note, high C, cannot be sustained on most instruments, or when it can, tends to be a ear-piercing shreak. It should be used only in a forte passage. Producing this note requires quite a burst of air for it to sound.

# *Alternate Fingering Studies*

Quite often the tempo at which a given piece of music can be played is limited by the presence of passages that, because of the difficulty of certain fingering combinations, can only be taken at a speed slower than desired. For instance, the following example is very awkward, more so for a right-handed person than a left, but awkward nonetheless:

Fingering-combination difficulties almost always involve the exchange of one finger for another, and these exchanges, although often unavoidable even at fast tempos, can range from moderately problematic to humanly impossible. There are a number of alternate fingerings available to the recorder player that will simplify many of these awkward combinations and render the unplayable playable.

Many professional player-teachers maintain that alternates are to be used only for trills or in extremely rare situations of great difficulty but otherwise should be avoided even by beginning players. The argument that most, or at least, many of these fingerings are less than desirable in terms of quality and intonation is, in general, valid but only in a relative sense. Where speed and accuracy are to be factors, the ultimate determinant must always be the playability of a given passage. Yes, the ideal is to use only the fingerings producing the best and most in-tune notes, but often some sort of compromise is demanded. Alternates used in contexts where they are not sustained are very valuable and necessary. Some of the available alternates are every bit as in tune as the "normal" fingerings. (Many of the players who decry the use of these fingering combinations can be seen to use them in concert situations in spite of what they maintain.)

Probably the most commonly used alternate is:

In the following exercises we will label the alternate fingerings with a capital A, and when a normal or regular fingering should be used, it will be labeled with a capital R.

Alternate B-natural for C recorders

Alternate E-natural for F recorders:

At slow tempos these exercises would not require the use of alternates; therefore, play them as fast as possible.

From these it can be seen that the alternate can be used to avoid finger exchanges in many musical contexts. For C recorders, if there is either an A-natural or a G-sharp on either side of the B, the regular (R) fingering should be used otherwise another finger exchange would be required. This would mean a D or C-sharp on either side of an E for F recorders.

Any of the following could (and in some cases, should) use the alternate.

Alternate E-naturals for C recorders - Alternate A-naturals for F recorders

Five different fingerings are available for the above notes. The first is considered to be the "normal" fingering but the next three can almost be considered as equal to the first in terms of utility and quality (on most instruments). The fifth fingering is a true alternate and will vary in quality from instrument to instrument, therefore it should only be used in situations where the note is not to be sustained. These fingerings, numbered one through five are:

1. ●●● | ●●○○ 2. ○●● | ●●○○ 3. ●●● | ●●○○ 4. ○●● | ●●○○ 5. ●●● | ●○●●

How is the choice made as to which of the fingerings is to be employed in a particular situation? With the exception of problems involved in finger exchanges, the principle that is paramount is that of economy of motion. In other words, the fewer number of fingers in motion, the better. If a combination can be effected using three fingers, that is better than moving four; if a combination can be played moving two fingers, that is preferable to moving three, and so forth.

Number 1 is probably the most used of the fingerings, and number 2 is used when the note is to be sustained as its quality may be best on some instruments. Numbers 3, 4, and five are used when the following combinations occur:

Quite often passages in a piece of music will requite two or more fingerings for the same note depending on context:

The above are merely suggestions but they include combinations that involve the least amount of finger motion.

The notes: 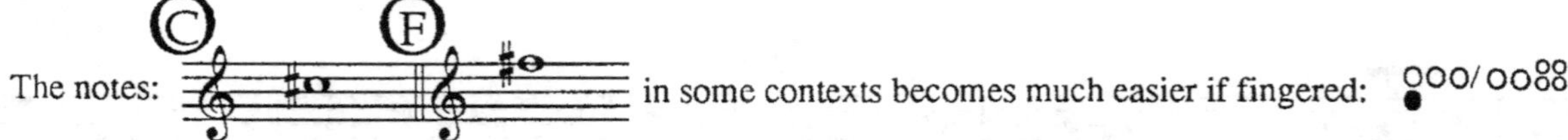 in some contexts becomes much easier if fingered:

This does away with the thumb and second finger exchange.
The exercises below will use R for the regular fingering and A for the alternate:

On most recorders the thumb fingering is as good a note as the regular fingering, so it may by sustained.

Possibly the most awkward area of fingering combinations on the recorder involves passages that include the notes:

Solutions to the many problems involving these notes require alternates, not only for these notes, but other notes going to, or coming from them, depending on context:

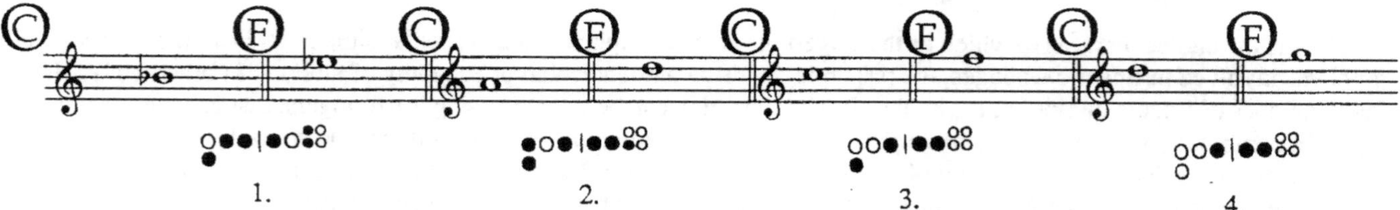


The following exercises explore some of the problem areas in dealing with these notes as well as solutions to those problems. The letter R will indicate the regular note and numbers will refer to alternate fingerings in the above chart:

Following is a set of exercises involving awkward note combinations that can be simplified by the use of special fingerings. Practice these very assiduously, getting them "under the fingers." They can be of great value in contexts where the success or failure of a particular piece depends on executing a passage where the normal fingerings are simply too awkward beyond a certain speed:

107. (8) A B

Etc. Etc.

A B

(8) C D

Etc. Etc.

(8) C D

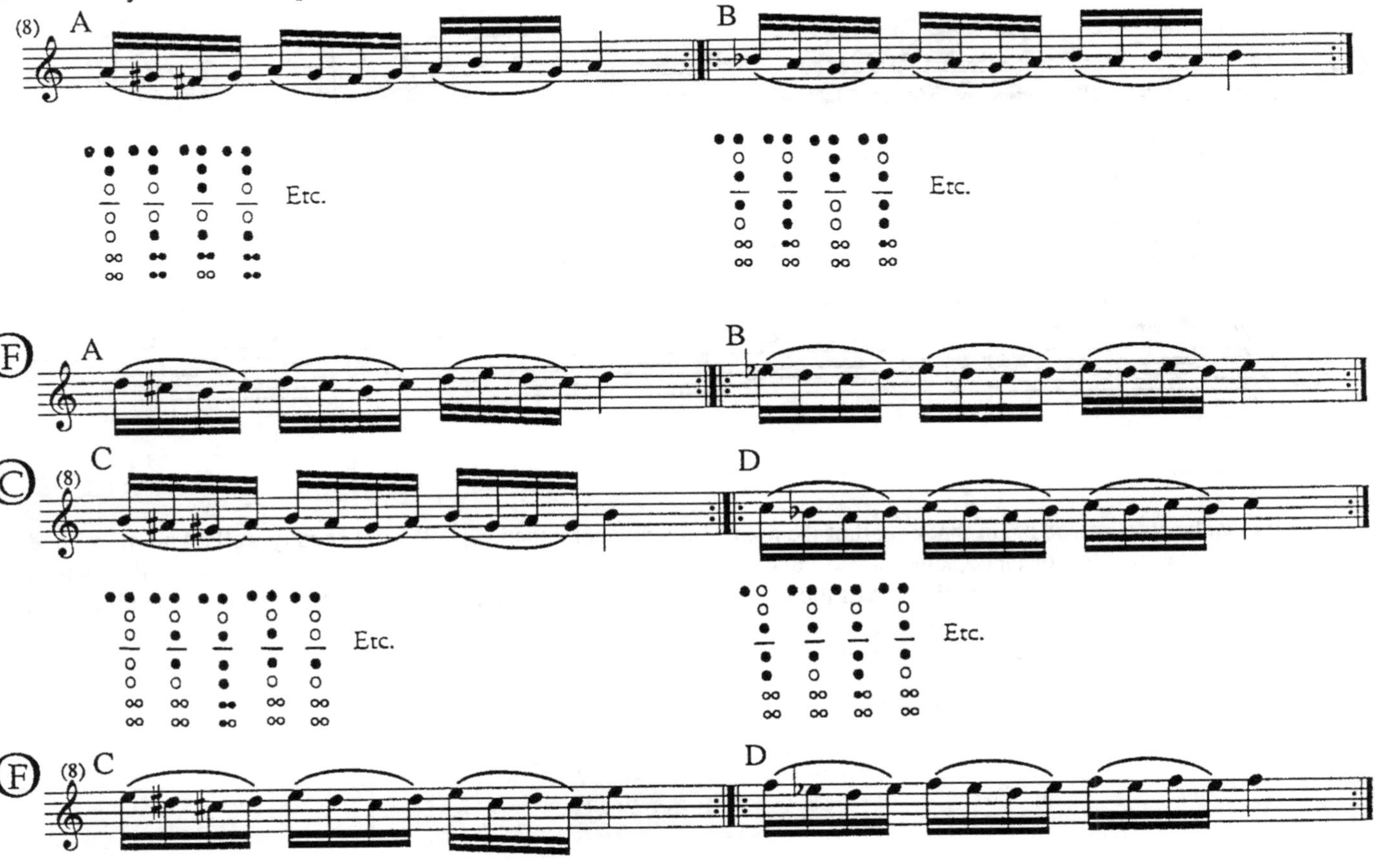

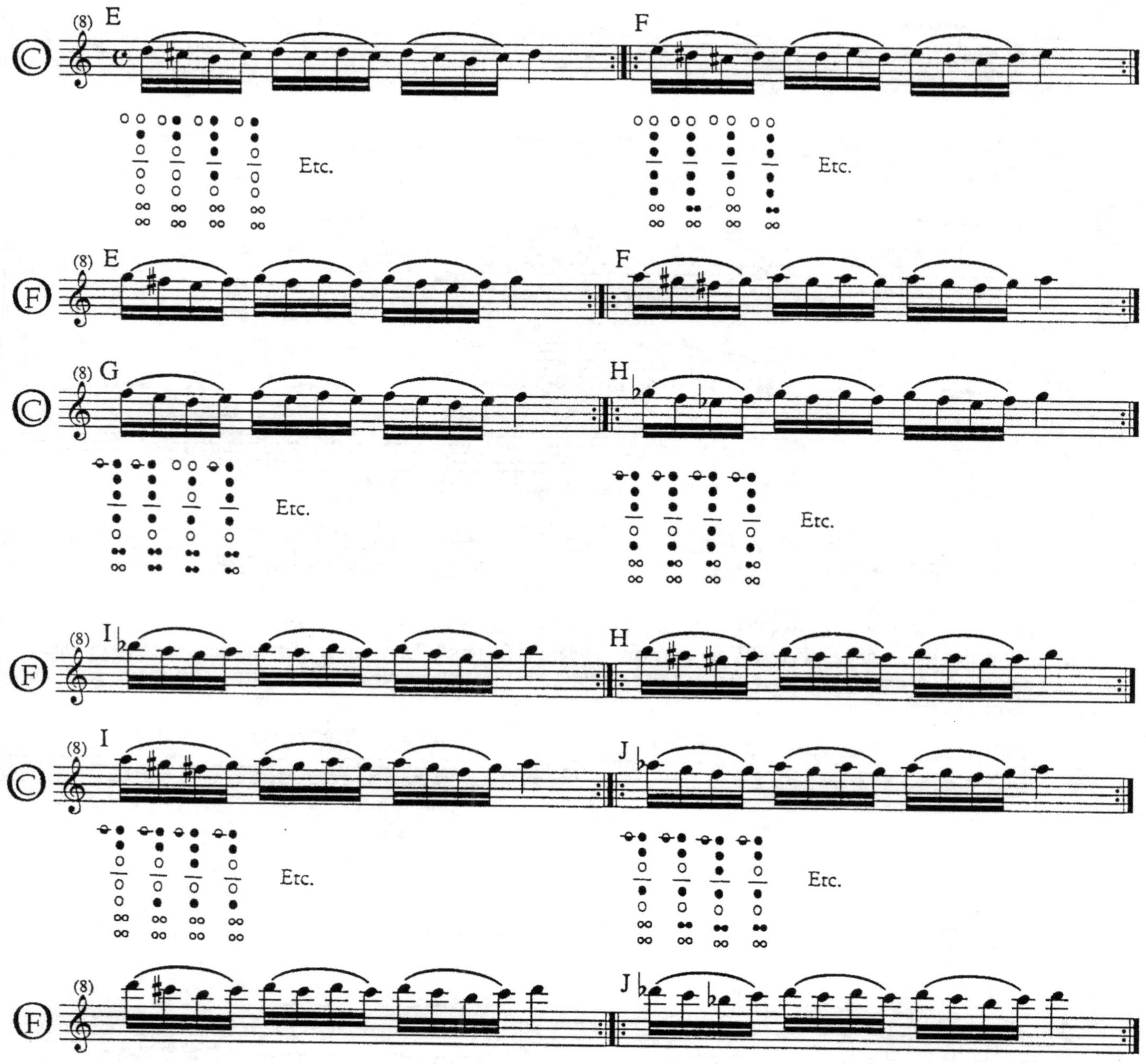


It must be emphasized again that not all of the above fingering combinations will work equally well on all makes and voices of recorders. For instance, letters I and J above might work quite well on your sopranino but not as well on your alto. You may have to experiment with the size of the half-hole thumb by pinching it off to a smaller aperture or making it larger.

# *Scale and Arpeggio Studies*

C
3.
(8)
F
4.
rit.
allargando

C
5.
(8)
rit.
F
6.
ritard.

C
(8)
7.
rit.
F
(8)
8.
rit.

Ⓒ (8)
9.

(8)

(8)

(8)

(8)

(8)

(8)
*rit.*

Ⓕ (8)
10.

(8)

(8)

(8)

(8)

(8)

(8)
*rit.*

C
(8)
11.
rit.
F
12.
rit.

C
13.
(8)
rit.
F
14.
(8)
rit.

C
15.
(8)
rit.
F
16.
rit.

C
17.
(8)
rit.
F
18.
rit.

(8)
19.
rit.
(8)
20.
rit.

(C)
21.
(8)
rit.
(F)
22.
(8)
rit.

C
23.
rit.
F
24.
senza rit.

C
25.
(8)
rit.
F
36.
rit.

C
27.
(8)
rit.
F
28.
rit.

C
29.
(8)
rit.
F
30.
rit.

C
31.
(8)
rit.
F
32.
(8)
rit.

C
33.
(8)
rit.
F
34.
rit.

C
(8)
35.
rit.
F
36.
senza rit.

37.
(8)
rit.
38.
rit.

The small numbers in the music refer to special fingerings in the chart at the bottom of each page. These alternates are valuable in that they help to avoid awkward finger exchanges or to avoid unnecessary finger motion in a repeated passage (particularly numbers 5, 6, 7, and 8 on this page).

E.
F.
G.
H.
1.
2.
3.
4.
5.
6.
7.
8.
9.
10.
11.

1. 2. 3. 4. 5.

# *Studies for the Bass Recorder*

3.
4.

5.
6.

7.
rit.
8.
senza rit.

9.
rit.
10.
rit.

11.
rit.
12.
rit.

13.
rit.
14.
rit.

8
15.
rit.
8
16.
rit.

# Vibrato

Vibrato is possibly the one musical technique that has generated the most debate and controversy among teachers and performers. Most voice teachers maintain that vibrato will occur naturally without any conscious muscular effort when a student achieves the correct breathing technique and develops the proper use of the vocal mechanism. With wind instruments, however, such as the oboe, flute, or recorder, there has to be some muscle or combination of muscles that, acting upon the airstream, will produce that pleasing (to most ears) undulation of tone that we call vibrato.

The two schools of thought regarding vibrato on the recorder may not necessarily be mutually exclusive as many players maintain. One group holds that vibrato is produced in the throat by opening and partially closing the glottis, while the other group maintains that vibrato should be the result of the so-called diaphragm muscles (actually the intercostal muscles) "squeezing" out pulses of air. Adherents of each of these systems are able to give convincing arguments in favor of each and demonstrate that each can work in a musically satisfying way. The answer to this seeming contradiction may well lie somewhere between the two systems in that a combination of the two may be what most players actually employ. From a truly pragmatic point of view, it really does not matter how a player thinks of the breathing mechanism in producing a vibrato as long as the result is desirable in terms of its musicality.

We shall approach the study of vibrato at first from a standpoint of a deliberate, conscious muscular effort. Articulate the syllabic sequence "Tah-Ha-Ha-Ha-Ha," which requires the stomach muscles (possibly reinforced by the throat muscles) to push out five pulses or pushes of air. Do not allow the glottis to stop the air stream after each syllable as this will result in what the Germans call a *bockstriller* or goat trill. While you are in the process of training the muscles, exaggerate the pulses to the point that the tone is a little rough and the vibrato is overly wide. When the muscles are trained and and the procedure becomes more automatic and free it will be a simple matter to refine the technique and produce a pleasing sound. Now play some scales using this five-pulse vibrato:

Make sure that the fifth pulse is not sustained longer than any of the other four but that it stops immediately. Remember to overdo the pulses at first; it is necessary to get the muscles working smoothly and evenly without any uncontrolled trembling in the resulting tone. Following each group with rests allows the muscles to relax and not become tired. Above all, be critical of your results and do not settle for anything less than an agreeably musical sound. After you are satisfied with your progress using the five-pulse vibrato, go on to a nine-pulse pattern:

When the nine-pulse vibrato becomes almost automatic and you no longer feel fatigued when employing this technique, play long-note scales and arpeggios using a continuous vibrato. Remember only by practicing daily (or at least relatively often) can you train the muscles to achieve truly satisfactory results.

Vibrato should not be something that is turned on when you start to play and turned off when you stop, like a light switch. It should be used for expressive purposes only. Experiment with varying the amplitude (width) and even the rate (speed) of the vibrato, minimizing it for certain notes or phrases, intensifying it at climax points, starting a tone straight and gradually bringing it in on certain sustained notes—in short, using it in a manner that will enhance a musical line rather simply being a wobble that is always present in your tone.

There is quite a bit of debate as to the appropriateness of using vibrato at all in pre-nineteenth century music. This is one controversy that the author is simply not going to address here. As you, as a recorder student are, most likely, working under the tutelage of an experienced teacher, the author will defer to the wishes of the instructor in this regard.

# Studies from the Works of J. S. Bach

These studies were adapted for for recorders from many different types of compositions. In some cases transpositions were necessary in order the suit the specific ranges of the indicated instruments.

## 1. Allegro from Sonata II for Organ

Soprano Recorder

## 2. *Allegro from Sonata No. 1 for Flute*

# 3. *Excerpt from Cantata No. 79*

# 4. *Gigue from Suite No. 3 for Orchestra*

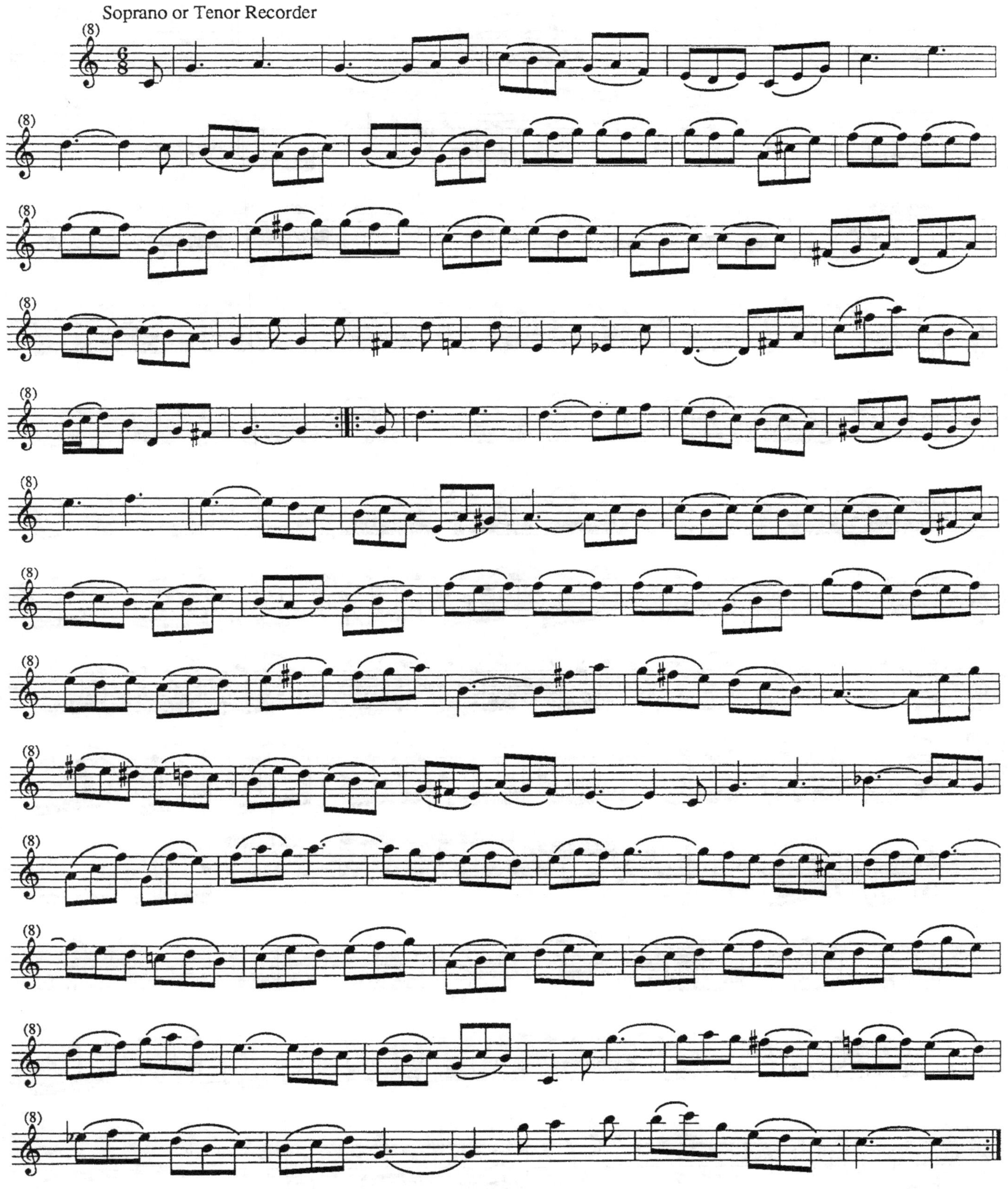

# 5. *Prelude from Partita No. 3 for Unaccompanied Violin*

*(Abridged)*

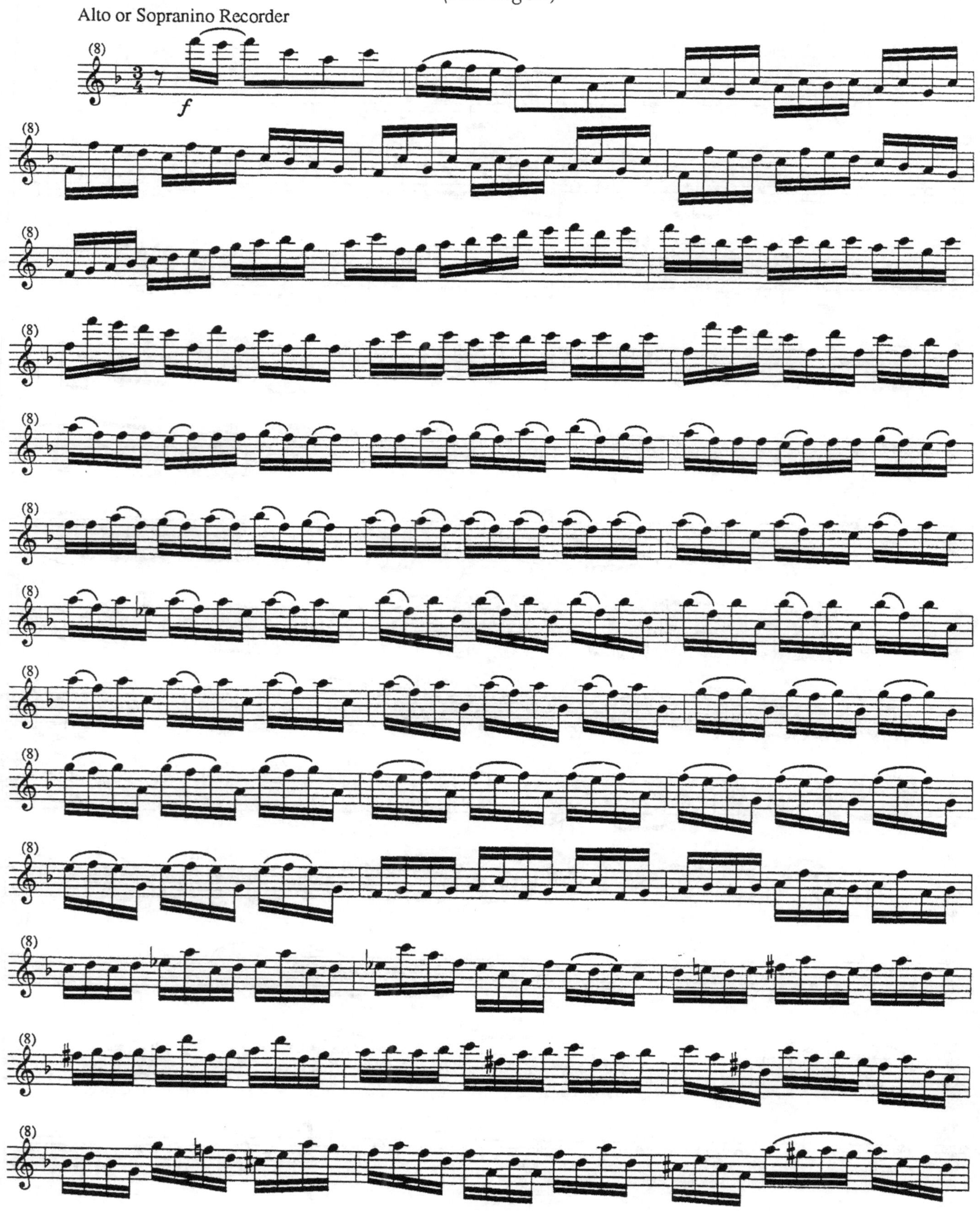

p
f
p
f
p
f
poco rit.

# 6. *Minuet and Badinerie from Suite No. 2 for Orchestra*

# 7. *Allemande from Cello Suite No. 4*

# 8. *Gigue from Cello Suite No. 3*

# 9. *Air and Bourrée from Suite for Orchestra No. 3*

# 10. Excerpt from Duetto, Cantata No. 48

# *11. Aria from Cantata No. 79*

# 12. *Aria from Cantata No. 59*

# Duos from the Works of J. S. Bach

## 1. Gigue from English Suite No. 2

* The alto recorder player must read the part up an octave.

# 2. *Bourrée from Lute Suite No. 1*

Soprano and Tenor Recorders

tr
rit.
rit.

# 3. *Bourrée from English Suite No. 1*

Alto and Tenor Recorders

# 4. *Minuet from French Suite No. 2*

Alto* and Bass Recorders

* Alto player must read an octave higher.

# 5. *Prelude from "The Well-Tempered Clavier"*

Soprano and Tenor Recorders

tr
(tr)
rit.

# 6. *Scherzo from Inventio Septima for Violin and B. C.*

# 7. *Bourrée from "Overture in the French Manner"*

## 8. *Gigue from Suite No. 3 (Lute?)*

Soprano and Alto Recorders

# 9. *Gavotte from English Suite No. 3*

Soprano and Alto Recorders

# 10. Minuet from English Suite No. 3

# 11. *Bourrée and Gigue from English Suite No. 3*

Tenor and Bass Recorders

T.

B.

# 12. Capriccio from Inventio Secunda

# 13. Aria from Cantata No. 46

tr

# *14. Aria from Partita No. 4*

Soprano and Tenor Recorders

# 15. Bourrée from French Suite No. 5

* Measured trill with *nachschlag*

# 16. Minuet from Anna Magdelena Bach's Notebooks

Alto and Bass Recorders

# *Renaissance Embellishment*

Performers in the Renaissance, both instrumentalists and singers, were not required to follow a written piece of music slavishly but were expected to embellish it with cadential ornaments, subtle and not so subtle melodic changes, as well as with rhythmic alterations. This infused the music with a feeling of spontaneity and freshness by the tasteful use of improvisatory practices. These practices were continued into the Baroque era but died out in the late eighteenth century. Composers often grumbled about the liberties taken with their compositions but performers continued to impose their own musical personalities on the music.

While it is true that to an early musician the process of embellishing a line of music was an essential part of his/her training to the point of becoming almost intuitive, later musicians were expected to reproduce only what was on the printed page—no more and certainly no less. Therefore, to perform a piece of early music so that it is stylistically close to what would been heard when it was created, a certain amount of embellishment must be added by the performer. Composers often left space, or set up certain musical situations, in order that performers would have leeway to exercise their own creative talents. Thus, composition in earlier times was a sharing of creative chores between the composer (who provided the basic framework of a work) with the interpretive skills of the performer.

It is safe to assume that all of the melodic and rhythmic devices that were available to the composer in the 16th century were also available to performers as they embellished a piece of music. By an analysis of a large body of music of the period in which variation techniques were employed, we can develop a set of rules and practices that can be applied, to some degree, to any given piece of music. With practice, any recorder player can approach music of the period with the same feeling for style as could any 16th-century musician.

This section of the method will deal with the seven principal devices of embellishment and ornamentation, exploring each progressively, analyzing different types of melodic contours, and applying different sets of practices in various ways to each.

## *1. Passing Tones*

A passing tone can be defined as a tone (or tones) that "fill in" an interval, in effect connecting two melodic tones. The usual interval involved is a third, there being but a single passing tone required to bridge the two given notes, but any interval larger than a third can be connected with passing tones.

Following are some examples demonstrating the use of the passing tone:

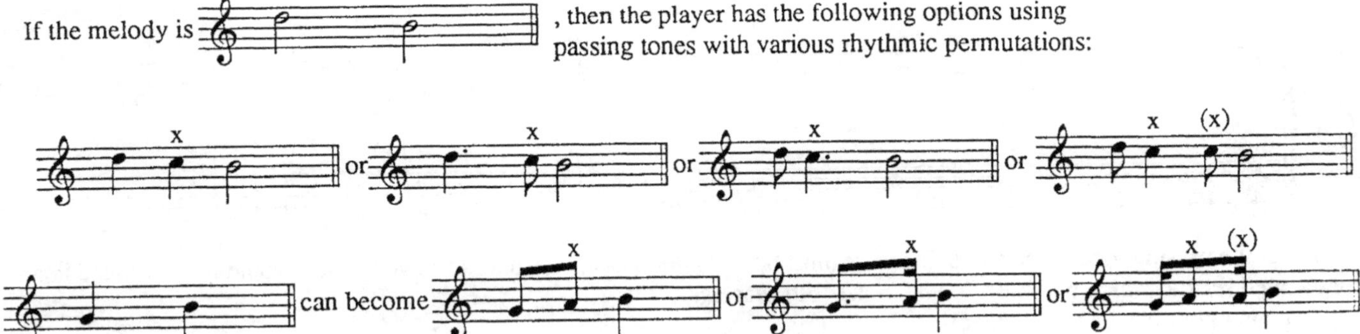


Note that this type of passing tone occurs only on a weak (unaccented) beat. Later we will be using accented passing tones that have different melodic and contrapuntal functions.

The above examples deal only with duple note values. The examples below show a few of the of the many possibilities in triple meter.

In the last example 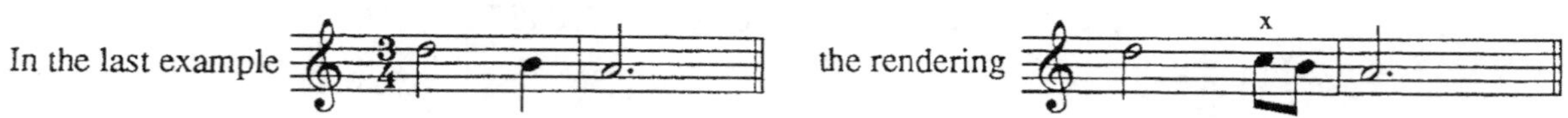 the rendering

would not be be correct if analyzed as an unaccented passing tone because it must be either on an unaccented beat or, if is beat is subdivided, the passing tone must be on the unaccented portion of that beat. However, the rendering shown above would be correct if analysed as an appoggiatura, one form of which is an accented passing tone.

More examples of passing tones are shown here:
Original melodic fragment

At this point the player might well ask "exactly when does one embellish a piece of music?" The one parameter that is impossible to reduce to a set of rules is that element which we must call "taste." Any set of melodic devices carried to an extreme is going to be less than satisfactory in performance. There are, however, a few guidelines that, if followed, can fit most musical situations and result in a reasonably tasteful effect:

1. All (or at least, most) cadences should be embellished in some manner.
2. Repeated sections should not be played the second time exactly the same as the first time but should be varied.
3. Repeated phrases, motives, and other melodic fragments should be varied.
4. Important thematic elements should not be obscured by too much embellishment the first time they are played.

The following duo should be played rather straight the first time with only a trill (or mordent) added on the last B.

On the repeat of the above melody there are several opportunities for passing tones in both parts. One possible embellishment of this could be:

Note that the passing tone in the fourth measure must be an F-sharp as the G-sharp followed by a F would have resulted in an augmented second which was not allowed in the 16th century.

Another possible embellishment is:

Notice that in neither of the above embellished examples are there passing tones in all of the possible melodic thirds; that would probably have been too much of one idea. Note also the passing tones filling in the interval of a fourth in the sixth measure of the second embellished version.

This example shows several possible problems, the principal one being that of tonality, or rather modality. The key signature would seem to indicate that this is in the key of C major or A minor and yet the beginning seems to be in G major. The third measure has a definite cadence on D (major or minor not specified) and the last measure cadences on A. The 16th-century scale systems were based on the earlier church-mode system that, in a sense, gave a certain amount of freedom in terms of intervallic relationships. For instance, in the example above, passing tones in the first two measures can include either F natural or F sharp. The piece starts in the mixolydian mode (G to G), cadences in the third measure in the dorian mode (D to D), and has a final cadence in the aeolian mode (A to A). Some modes allow for an ascending form that differs from its descending form. This example uses the ascending form of the mode in the first measure (the F natural) and the descending form in the second measure (the F sharp). The rules governing these two forms are not hard and fast, so whichever sounds better can be used.

Here is one embellished version using passing tones:

Following is a number of exercises to be embellished with passing tones. Play each several times, experimenting with various ways of using passing tones. Do not be afraid to change rhythms if the results are pleasing.

3.

4.

5.

6.

Suggested embellished versions of numbers three through six will be shown on the next two pages.

Before presenting embellished versions of exercises three through six, let us see exactly what the church modes are and what kinds of cadences are common in each.

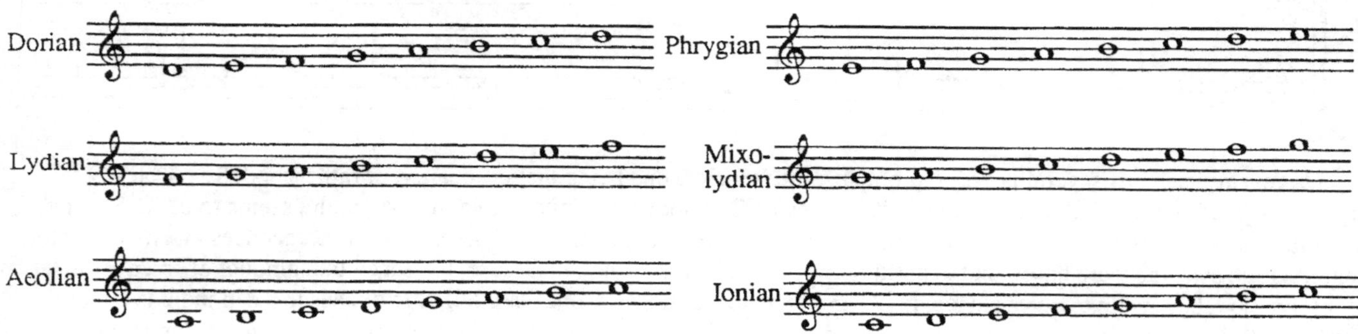


In the dorian mode there can be a possible C sharp functioning as a leading tone to the final D. The B might, on occasion, be flatted in order to avoid a tritone (augmented fourth or diminished fifth) which was a forbidden interval either melodically or between voices. The mixolydian and aeolian modes could also include a raised leading tone. In the aeolian mode, if the leading tone was approached by step from below, the F would also have to be sharped otherwise another forbidden interval, the augmented second, would occur. In the lydian and ionian modes the raised leading tones are built in.

The phrygian mode never uses a raised leading tone but rather has its own special type of cadence forms which can have a raised third but this is optional:

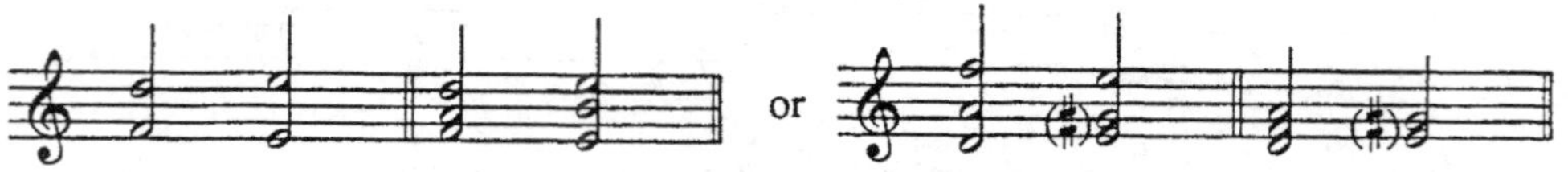


Most often the "minor" modes, where the interval between the root and third of the mode is a minor third, had a raised third (the so-called "Picardy third") on the final cadence of a piece as theoretical writers considered the minor third to be too "imperfect" an interval with which to end a piece. The dorian, phrygian, and aeolian modes were the ones affected by this practice. Ending with a minor chord became common in the 17th century although, even as late as the time of J. S. Bach, some composers, on occasion, still used the raised third on the last chord of a minor piece. All of the above modes could be transposed to other key centers although, in the 17th century, it was rare for a key signature to have moe than three flats or sharps.

The above is a rather simplified and truncated course in 16th-century modal contrapuntal usage but it will help explain some of the practices that we will be exploring in this embellishment study.

Now, let us try some of the possible embellished versions of numbers three through six using passing tones:

With a B flat in the signature, E flats throughout, and a final cadence on C, this piece can be considered to be in the dorian mode (D to D transposed down one tone). There is a cadence on G (transposed aeolian) in the fourth measure. The use of passing tones is fairly straightforward and not all of the melodic thirds have been "filled in" which might be a bit too much. Most often cadential trills or other such ornaments were not notated in the 16th century but were usually added by the performer as a matter of course. The last measure in the soprano part might be played:

or simply an unmeasured trill.

This piece is in a transposed mixolydian mode (in this case D to D, with an F sharp) with a cadence to the dorian in the fourth measure. The D in the second measure of the top part cannot be followed by a passing tone as this would result in parallel fifths with the lower part, which would be taboo.

This piece goes through two modal centers before it finally cadences in the aeolian. The first measure is in a mixolydian mode on F with an ascending E flat and a descending E natural. The second measure cadences in D, which looks like the phrygian mode (considering the key signature) but it cannot be as there is no leading tone in the phrygian mode. We can only conclude that this is a dorian cadence in C or an aeolian cadence in F.

This example starts in mixolydian, cadences in the second measure in the aeolian and has a final cadence in the ionian (D major). In actuality, the original versions of these fragments included some passing tones but, for our purposes, we are only going to concern ourselves, in terms of embellishment, with what is added by the performer.

## 2. *Neighboring Tones*

Neighboring tones (also called auxiliaries) are notes that lie diatonically either above or below a given note. As with neighboring tones, they must be used only on unaccented or weak beats. They must return to the principal note before progressing on. We will use a lowercase n to label them.

Examples:

In each of the above examples the neighboring tone moves opposite to the flow of the melody. That is, when the note that the melody is going to is higher, the neighboring tone will go down, and vice versa. This is not necessarily a rule, but it seems more musically satisfying that way. Let us look at examples a through d above with the neighboring tones reversed:

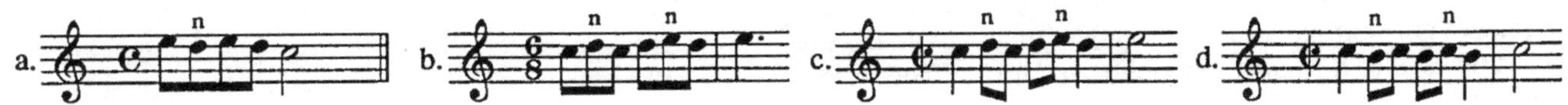

While each of the previous four neighboring-tone realizations is technically correct, and under certain melodic circumstances a reversal of the usual practice might be desired, the most musical solution of the problem is found in the first set of renderings. The exception to the common practice occurs if the interval involved is greater than a second in either direction, then the neighboring tone can go either way.

There are a large number of possible renderings of the above fragments using various rhythms and having the neighboring tones go either up or down. Here are ten variants on letter e above:

These are only a few of the many possibilities of this three note melodic fragment. Note that triplets are not usually mixed with duple divisions of a note in the same melodic or contrapuntal context. Note that in all of the above examples, the principal notes of the melody occur on the strong beats (beats one and three) and the main note must be restated before moving on to the next main note. In other words, the second note, A, must be preceded by a C and the third note by an A.

Here are some practice duos in which to add some neighboring tones:

One factor must be kept in mind when embellishing a piece of music is that it is possible inadvertently to commit one or another of the "sins" of correct usage when changing a given line. Parallel unisons, seconds, fourths, fifths, sevenths, or octaves are simply wrong in this style. In addition, the tritone and augmented second should be avoided although the tritone can be used as a passing or neighboring tone. These trangressions will occur and the solution is not to do something wrong a second time.

From playing through the above example, it is apparent that there are some excellent opportunities for the use of passing tones as well as neighboring tones. Following is a version of number eight using both types of embellishment devices:

The combination of passing tones with neighboring tones can result in some very desirable musical possibilities.

This fragment, 1. can be embellished the following ways using only the two types of devices:

1.a 1.b 1.c 1.d

This fragment, 2. can be embellished as follows:

2.a 2.b 2.c 2.d

9.

9.A

At this point it is necessary for the student to experience a number of pieces in various meters. The duos that follow will have no embellished versions so you are on your own. Use only the two types of devices covered so far.

Remember to use a trill on leading tones at cadences even when they are not so indicated.

### *3. The Appoggiatura*

For the purposes of this study, we will use two classes or types of appoggiatura, which we will label with a capital A. The first of these is the accented passing tone (x). This type differs from the regular passing tone in that it delays the sounding of the notated note.

This shows the difference in function between accented and unaccented passing tones. In example a.1 the written notes E and C sound a half beat later than notated, whereas, using passing tones, they sound where originally notated.

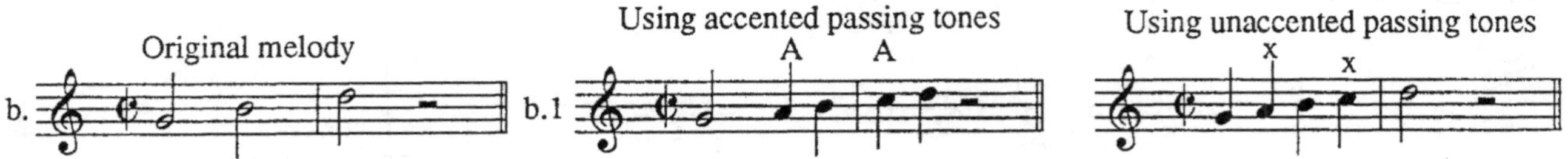


The second type of appoggiatua involves a leap (an interval greater than a second) to a tone on either side of the notated pitch, on a strong beat, and finally a resolution to the indicated note on a weak beat.

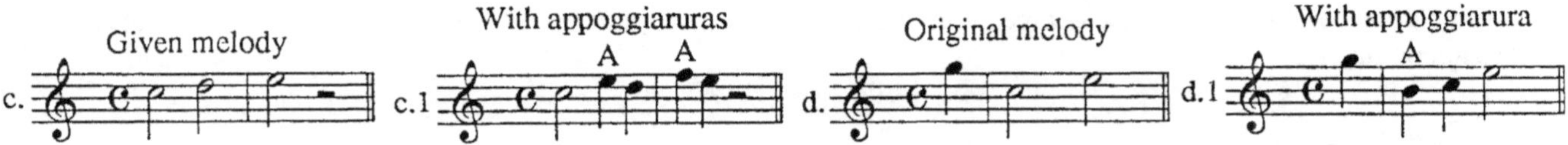


This type of appoggiatura has to be handled rather gingerly as too much of its use sounds overly mannered and stilted.

Embellish the following using only the two types of appoggiaturas even though the sound might become too predictable and repetitious.

There are some possible pitfalls in number 15. The tritone (augmented fourth or diminished fifth) cannot be articulated but can be used in passing or as neighboring tone. Granted, some of the errors are unavoidable when two or more players are freely embellishing a piece, but you should be aware of the sound of the incorrect practices and avoid them whenever possible. Another point to be made is the fact that, if there is more than one player on each part, embellishment cannot be used as the result would be chaotic (unless the players agree beforehand to do the same devices at the same places in the music). The one exception to this general rules is at cadence points where trills are demanded. Following is a realization of number 15 using appoggiaturas:

One problem will arise when one player decides to use unaccented passing tones and the other player opts for accented passing tones:

The resulting parallel seconds, of course, completely wrong and the ear should immediately hear the clash. Therefore, it is wise to leave the bulk of the embellishment chores to the uppermost part and only to embellish the under parts when it appears safe to do so. In a multi-voice composition, the bass voice employs little embellishment and never (or rarely) employs appoggiaturas.

16.

16.A

At this point it would be wise if the second part become more limited in its embellishment, leaving the upper free to improvise. An occasional passing or neighboring tone should suffice in the lower part.

Note the pattern of the neighboring tone followed by appoggiatura in the above example. Now go back and play exercises one through sixteen using all of the embellishment types studied so far.

## *4. Anticipations*

An anticipation is a type of nonharmonic tone that becomes harmonic when another voice resolves. By definition it is simply a tone that "anticipates" the tone to which it is moving. This movement must always be by step. We will use a lowercase a to label them"

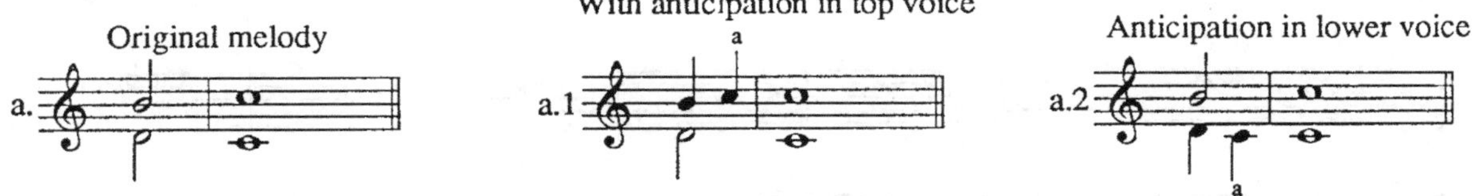


The second beat in a.1 and a.2 above are dissonant sevenths that become consonant octaves after the bar line when the half note moves to the whole note.

The two things to keep in mind when using this type of embellishment are (1) the anticipation must proceed in a scale-wise motion, either up or down, and (2) there must be no harmonic change at the same time as the anticipation.

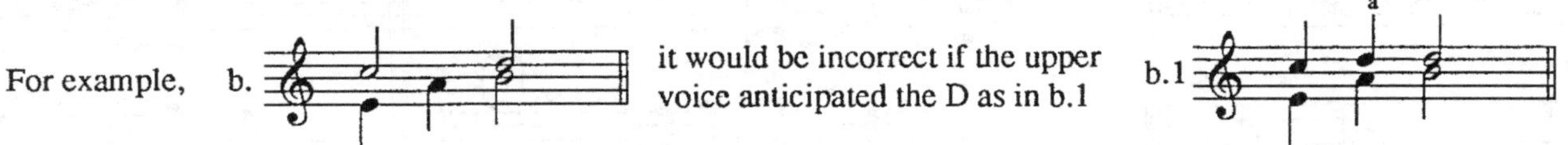


Watch for passages in parallel thirds or sixths as these lend themselves to nice "chains" of anticipations and resolutions:

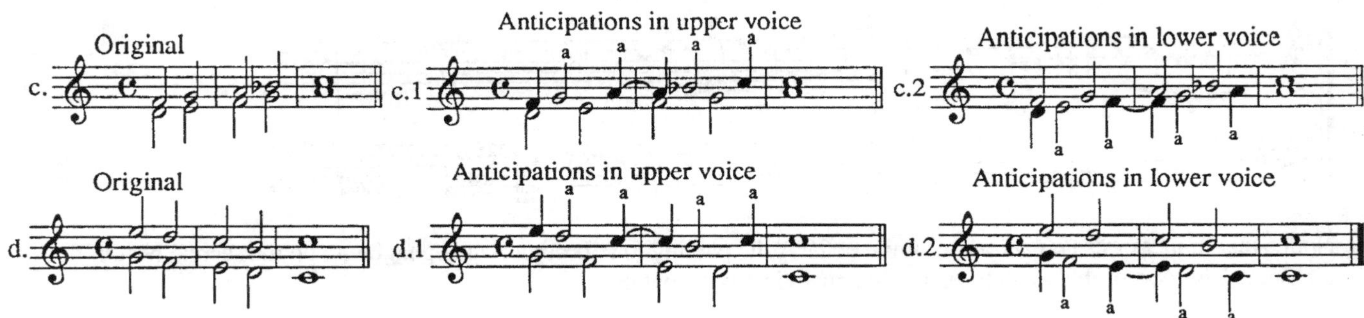

18.

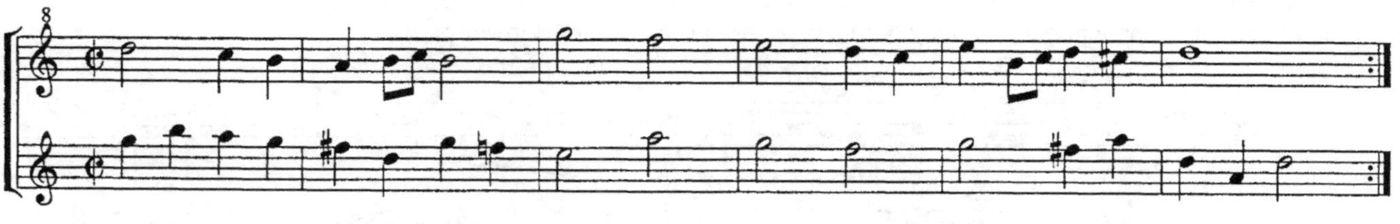

18.A

Remember to avoid using anticipations when there is motion in the other part at the same time.

19.

19.A

In number twenty apply all of the embellishment devices that we have explored so far.

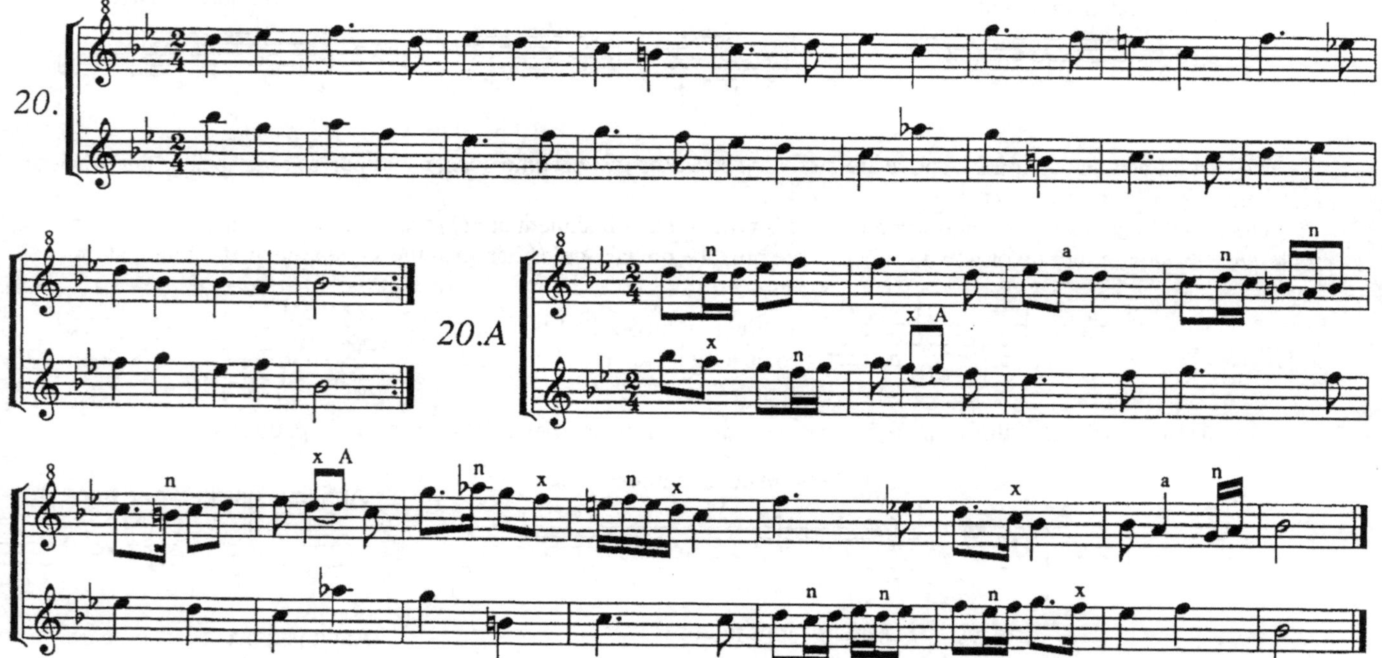


Notice that in measures two and six of number 20.A the passing tone becomes an appoggiatura on the second beat of the measure. This sort of thing can happen when there is a syncopation.

## 5. *Suspensions*

A suspension functions in a manner exactly opposite to an anticipation. The anticipation arrives at a note earlier than indicated and a suspension delays its arrival. We will us a capital S to label suspensions.

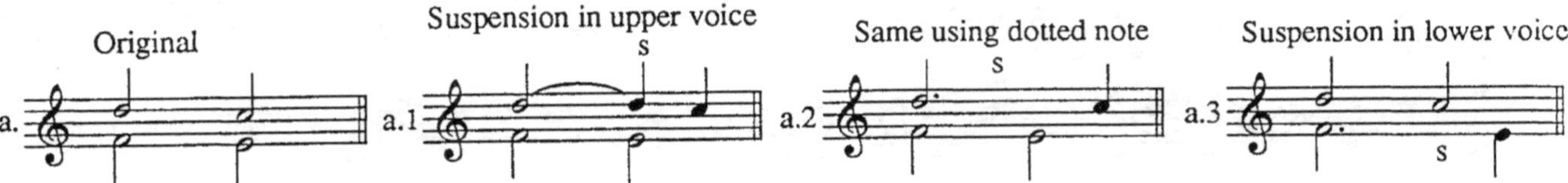


As with the anticipation, the motion must be stepwise. Sometimes a combination of the two types can be effective:

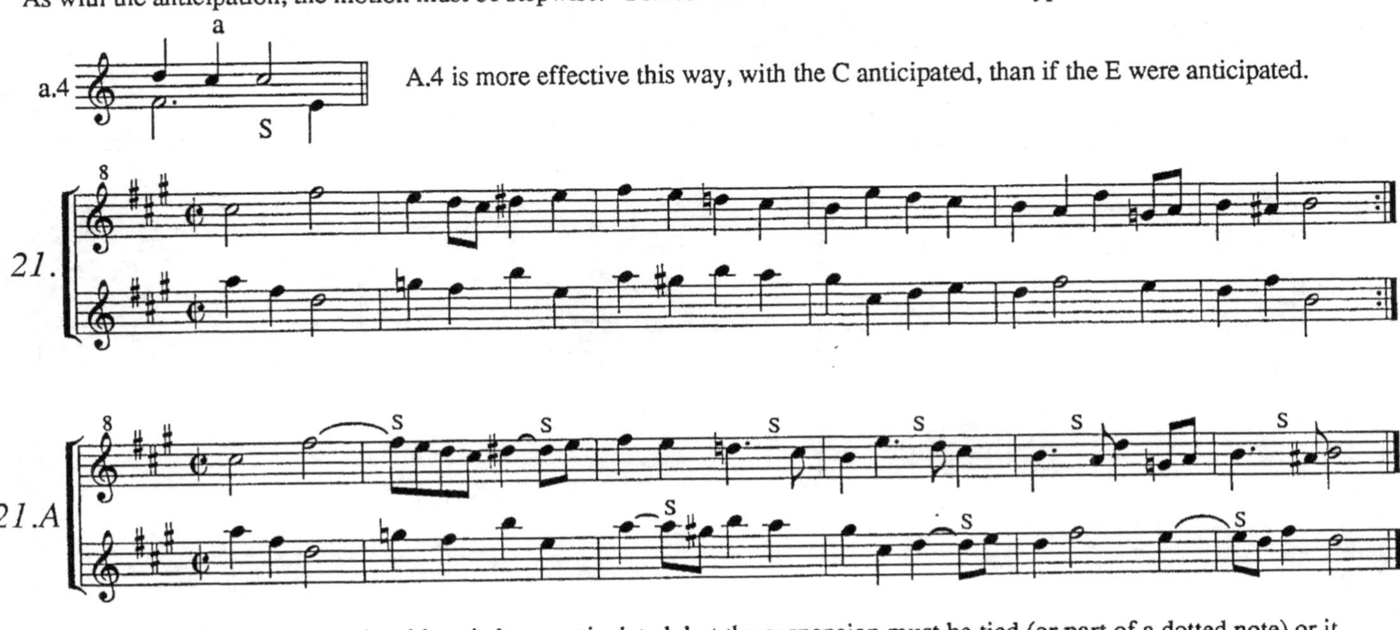


A.4 is more effective this way, with the C anticipated, than if the E were anticipated.

Note that the anticipation can be either tied or rearticulated, but the suspension must be tied (or part of a dotted note) or it becomes an appoggiatura.

Notice that in measure six of number 22.A the suspension is prolonged so that both voices do not move at the same time. There are no embellishments in the lower part in 22. or 22.A but try the following alternate with the upper part in both.

Now go back and apply these embellishments to numbers one through twenty.

In number 23 use all of the devices (passing tones, upper and lower neighboring tones, both types of appoggiaturas, and suspensions) that we have covered so far.

23.

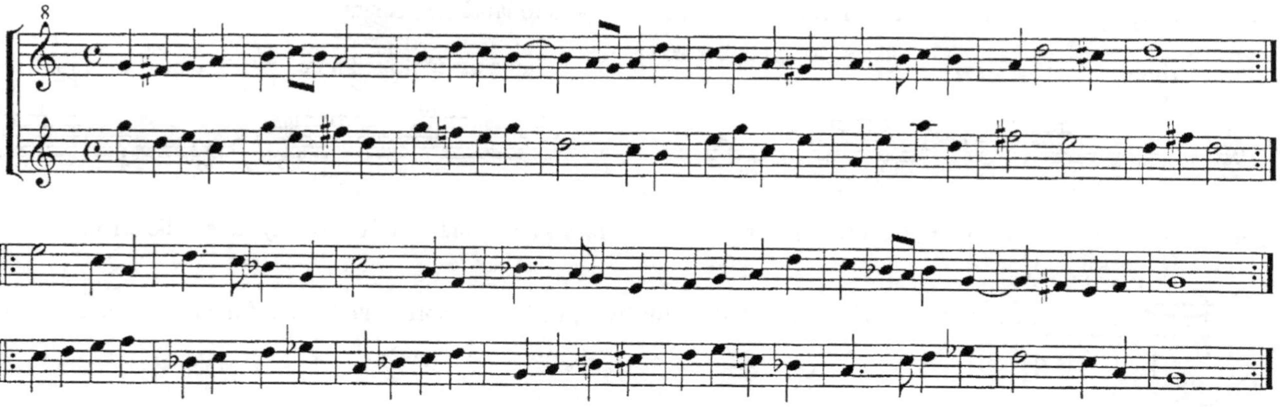

23.A

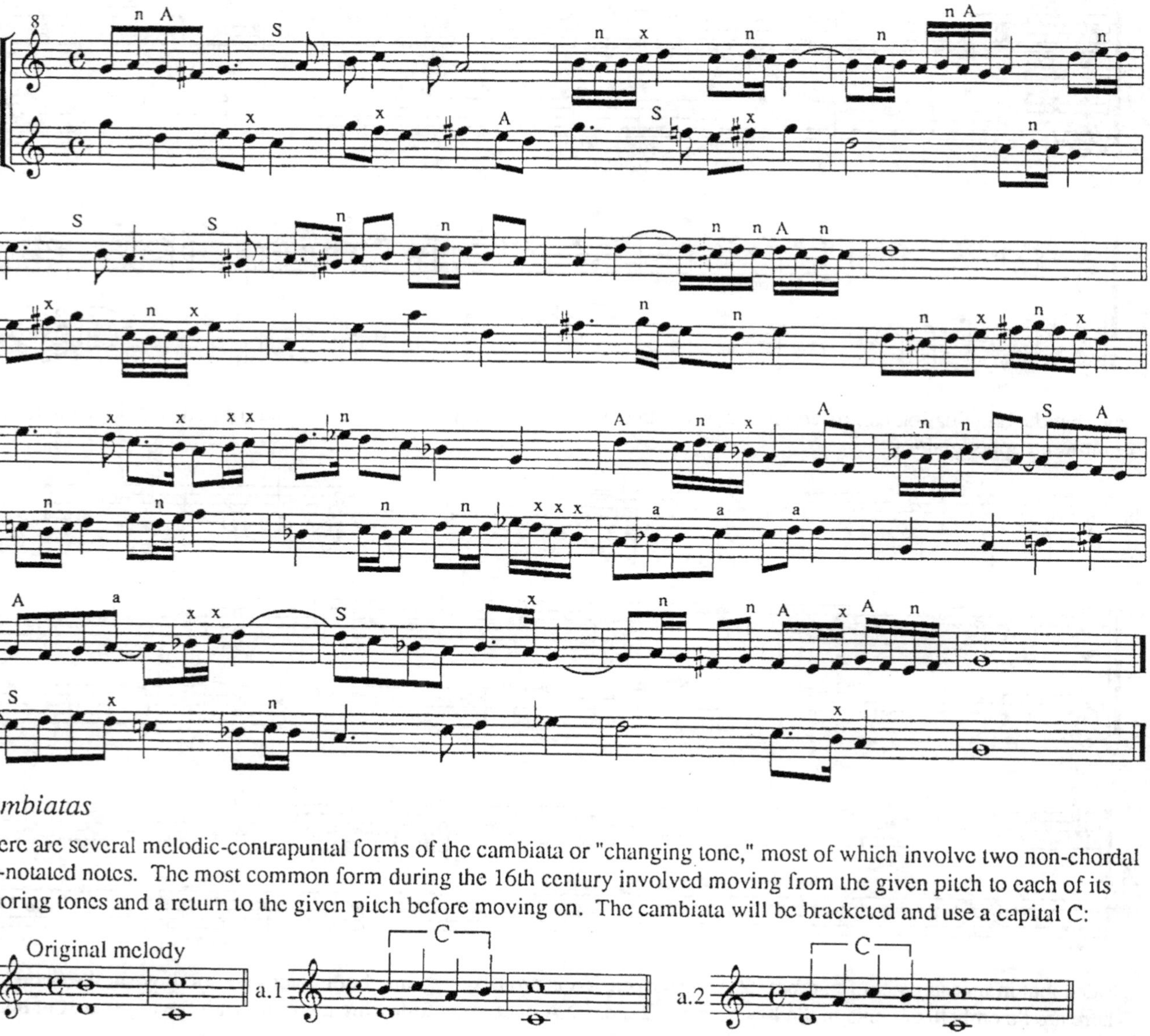

## 6. *Cambiatas*

There are several melodic-contrapuntal forms of the cambiata or "changing tone," most of which involve two non-chordal or non-notated notes. The most common form during the 16th century involved moving from the given pitch to each of its neighboring tones and a return to the given pitch before moving on. The cambiata will be bracketed and use a capital C:

The following show how the cambiata patterns can be used with different types of melodic contours. These are not trios but consist of only two parts. The middle part is an embellishment on the upper line and the bottom part is the actual second (alto) voice.

24\. A. Original melody — B. — With cambiatas — Alto part

C. — D.

E.

Remember that the above are only examples. Any of the embellishment devices can be taken to extremes by overuse. In number 25 use as many of the cambiata contours as possible. Avoid any parallel octaves or fifths. An occasional fourth or even second can be tolerated if they pass quickly and are not on accented beats.

## 7. *The Échapée*

The échapée or "escape tone" involves a leap away from a nonharmonic tone according to certain stylized melodic patterns. The earliest form of this figure was based on the interval of a descending fourth. We will use a capital E with which to label the échapée.

Occasionally, but rarely, it involved the ascending fourth:

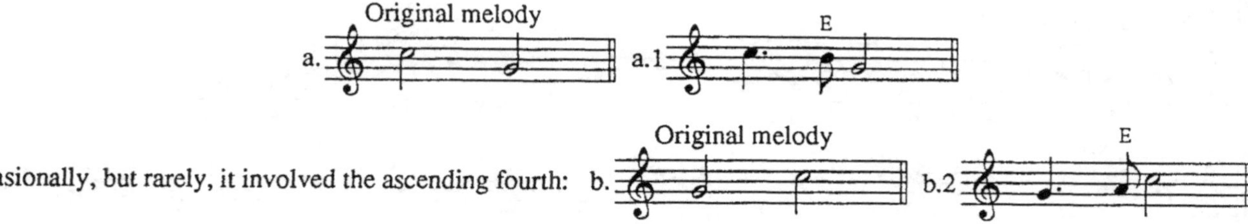


Later the escape-tone idea developed into the following forms or types:

These forms (c.1, c.2, d.1, e.1), although they were occasionally used by composers in the 16th century, did not really become important melodic devices until late in the 18th century.

Notice the principal differences between the forms of the cambiata and those of the échapée. In the cambiata the non-chordal tone proceeds to a chordal tone by step, either ascending or descending, while in the échapée the non-harmonic tone proceeds to the next harmonic tone by leap.

Although we refer to non-chordal or nonharmonic tones with regard to the échapée, there are instances when the escape tone is actually not nonharmonic at all, being fully consonant with the other voice, as in the penultimate bar of 25.A; nevertheless from the stand point of melodic embellishment, it remains an échapée.

The duos on the next page should be played through many times. Start by embellishing with passing tones only, gradually adding each type of device until all seven have been used. Remember that facility comes only with experience.

27.

28.

### *8. Free Embellishment*

Free embellishment has to do with all the other devices and processes that do not fall into the previous seven categories. It is essentially the process of improvisation. While it may include many or all of the seven devices, its main premise is based on realizing and dealing with the basic harmonic structure rather than a given melody. In this concept it is closer to the ethos of jazz creation in that the performer is free to invent completely new melodies based, not on a given melody, but on the stated or implied harmonic progression of a piece.

In order to improvise on (or freely embellish) a melody the performer should be aware of exactly what the harmonic basis of a given piece of music is. The following duet has been analyzed as to its implied harmonic structure using the figurations commonly employed in undergraduate college theory. This system is usually employed with tonal (rather than modal) pieces we are going to assume, for the sake of the analysis, that this is in the key of G major (rather than mixolydian mode).

Although we are dealing only with intervallic relationships in this pavan-like piece, its harmonic implications are fairly clear-cut. Number 29 presents two variations on the harmonic structure. In analyzing these you will find all of the seven embellishment types being used but not with any relationship to the original melody. This should not be performed as a trio as there are some parallel seconds and other breaches of good part writing between the two soprano parts.

29.A

29.B

# *Baroque Embellishment*

Embellishment in the baroque era was not a matter of supplanting the practices of the renaissance but rather of adding to them certain stylized ornaments that were indicated by signs placed before, over, or after a note to tell the performer more or less what the composer wanted at a given point in the music. "More or less" because not all ornamental signs meant the exact same thing to all players or singers. A particular sign might be realized one way to a German musician, another way by a French performer, and be meaningless to someone in England. Because of this confusion, and because he wanted tighter control over the performances of his music, J. S. Bach took to notating everything he wanted with only minimal use of ornamental signs, particularly in his later keyboard pieces. The signs themselves, for the most part, represented devices that composers and performers had been employing during the renaissance and constituted a sort of musical shorthand that required fewer strokes of the pen.

An ornament can be more than simply an embellishment on a note; it can be truly thematic. Can one imagine Bach's glorious D-minor toccata without the initial mordent?

The following table of ornaments, although far from complete, shows the most commonly used embellishments in the baroque period:

## *1. The Trill*

The trill can take many forms, both measured and unmeasured, with and without the nachschlag (terminating notes), and could be maintained for the full duration of a note, or only part of it. The usual sign employed was tr. but often composers would use a simple + sign. Remember that trills in this period did not start on the indicated note but rather with the upper neighboring tone, in effect, starting with an appoggiatura. The following examples are of measured trills:

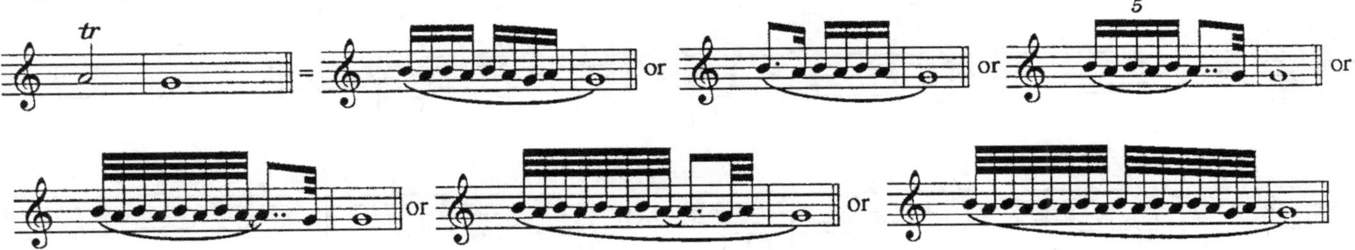


## *2. The Mordent*

The mordent is a simple ornament consisting of a dip from the indicated note to its lower neighboring tone and then immediately back to the main pitch. This must be executed on the beat, not before it:

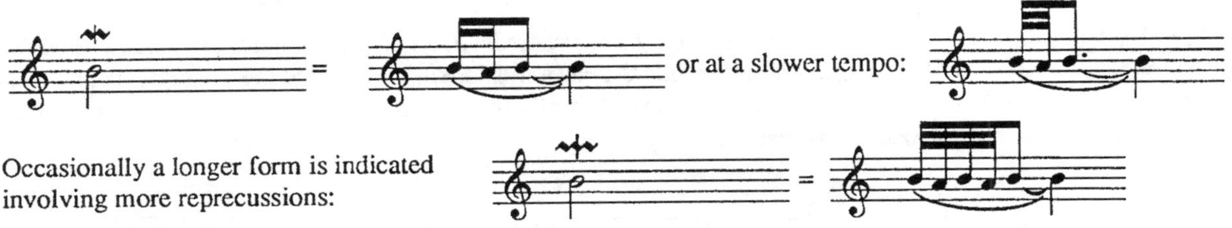


Occasionally a longer form is indicated involving more reprecussions:

## *3. The Pralltriller*

The pralltriller is a short trill starting with the upper auxillary and usually consisting of four notes, although a longer form was called for on occasion (as with the longer form of the mordent):

## *4. The Coulé*

The coulé or "slide" is an ornament that Bach used several times and consists of a run u ® a given note. The interval spanned was, most often, a third although it could be a fourth or even a fifth. As with most ornaments it occurs on the beat:

## *5. The Appoggiatura*

The appoggiatura as a function has been covered in the section on renaissance embellishment and, during the baroque era, some new notational devices developed to indicate this ornament. Modern editions of baroque music where the appoggiatura is called for too often realize it incorrectly according to what is known of the practice of the time. Our two main sources of information as to the interpretation of the various types of appoggiatura are the keyboard method of C. P. E. Bach (1714-1788) and the flute method of J. J. Quantz (1697-1773), both written during the 18th century.

The rules governing the appoggiatura are:

1. The appoggiatura takes half of the value of a note that can be divided into two equal parts (a. through e., below).
2. On a dotted note (divisible into three parts) the appoggiatura takes two-thirds of the value (f. and g., below).
3. On a note that is tied, the appoggiatura is maintained, resolving on the second note (letter h., below).

When small notes are used to indicate the appoggiatura it does not matter what note value is used for the small note—half, quarter, or eighth—the realization remains the same.

C. P. E. Bach and J. J. Quantz had differing views on the correct realization of the passing appoggiatura. Bach's interpretation was that of the older renaissance style while Quantz's was looking forward to the classical era and what was to become the grace note (a short note played before the beat). Actually the example below contains two accented passing tones and one appoggiatura that is approached by leap.

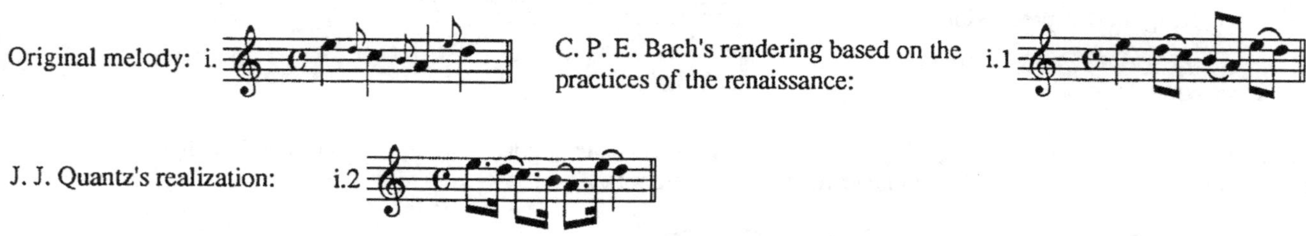


From the above example, we can see that there were areas of disagreement even among very knowledgeable musicians of the period—which can cast doubt on some aspects of the "rules."

Some composers, among them J. S. Bach, often used little hook signs, rather than small notes, to denote an appoggiatura. The rules remain the same. These signs are used for both the ascending and descending appoggiaturas, the placement of which determined the type it was to be:

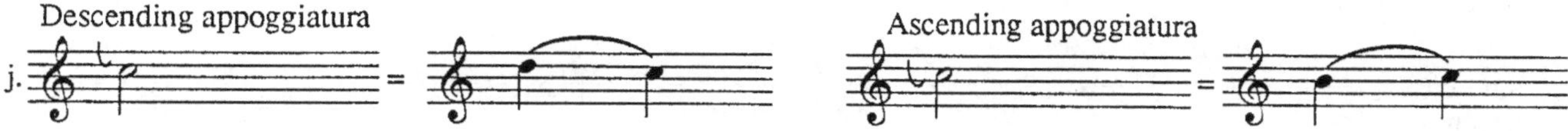


## *6. The Turn*

The turn is an ornament that starts on a neighboring tone, moves through the indicated note to the opposite neighboring tone and returns to the main note. There are several forms of the turn as well as inversions of each:

Sometimes composers would place the turn sign between notes indicating a different usage:

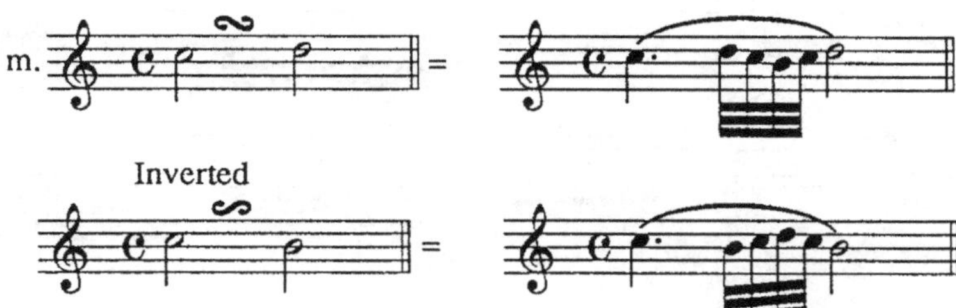


At faster tempos or with shorter note values, the turn could be a simple four-note figure:

Following a dotted note (in simple meter) the turn would take the following form:

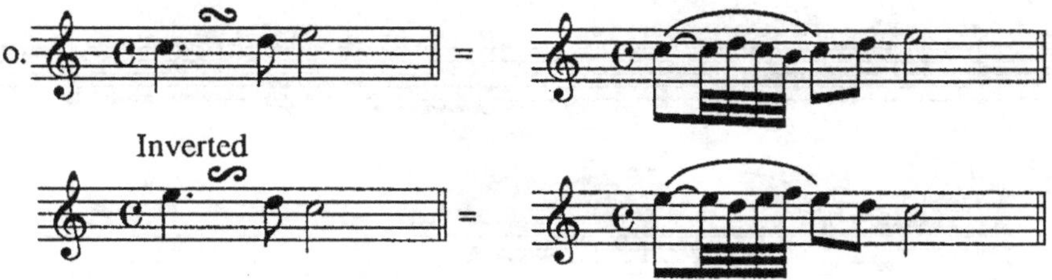


The foregoing constitute some of the principal ornament types of the baroque era. There were many others and if the student wishes to pursue this further the are a number of fine music dictionaries that provide a more complete exposure to this subject.

The following is the first movement of G. F. Handel's sonata for alto recorder with a suggested embellished version.

# *Sonata in C Major*

*First Movement*

13
tr
3
3
tr
15
tr
3
3
tr
3
3
tr
17
19
21
23
Adagio
rit.
Cadenza
6
tr

## *Double and Triple Tonguing*

Tonguing notes on the recorder, or indeed, on any wind instrument is the interruption of the air stream by the use of the tongue so that notes are separated to some degree. The physical process employed in double and triple tonguing produces a reflex or rebounding of the tongue that results in more than one articulation. Using this technique the tongue is capable of a much faster motion and, as a result, faster notes can be produced. A syllabic approach is the usual method employed to produce this effect. For double tonguing a brass player uses the unvoiced syllables "tah-kah, tah-kah" or "too-koo, too-koo" and "tah-tee-kah, tah-tee-kah" or "too-too-koo, too-too-koo" for triple tonguing. These syllables tend to be rather explosive when used on the recorder, so most players use "duh-guh" for double and "duh-dee-guh" for triple tonguing. Other players have success using "doo-dle, doo-dle" for double and "doo-dle-doo, doo-dle-doo" for triple, or some variant on these such as "duh-dle, duh-dle" and "duh-dle-duh, duh-dle-duh." Some experimentation which will work best for the individual player.

The tempos on the following exercises will have to be brisk enough so that the player does not fall back into single tonguing. Strive for smoothness and, above all, evenness:

Ⓒ (8) *1.*

Ⓕ (8) *2.*

Ⓒ (8) *3.*

Ⓕ (8) *4.*

Be very critical of your results. The double- or triple- tongued notes must be even in terms of duration and articulation. It may be necessary at first to stress the rebound notes slightly in order to make them of an equal degree of articulation.

C
(8)
5.
F
6.
C
7.
F
8.
C
9.
F
10.
C
11.

C
F
(8)
12.
C
(8)
sim.
13.
F
(8)
sim.
14.
C
F
(8)
sim.
15.
C
F
(8)
16.
C
(8)
17.
C
F
(8)
18.

(8)
19.
3
(8)
(8)
20.
3
(8)
(8)
21.
3
(8)
(8)
22.
3
(8)
(8)
23.
3
(8)
(8)
24.
3
(8)
(8)
25.
(8)

Bass Recorder

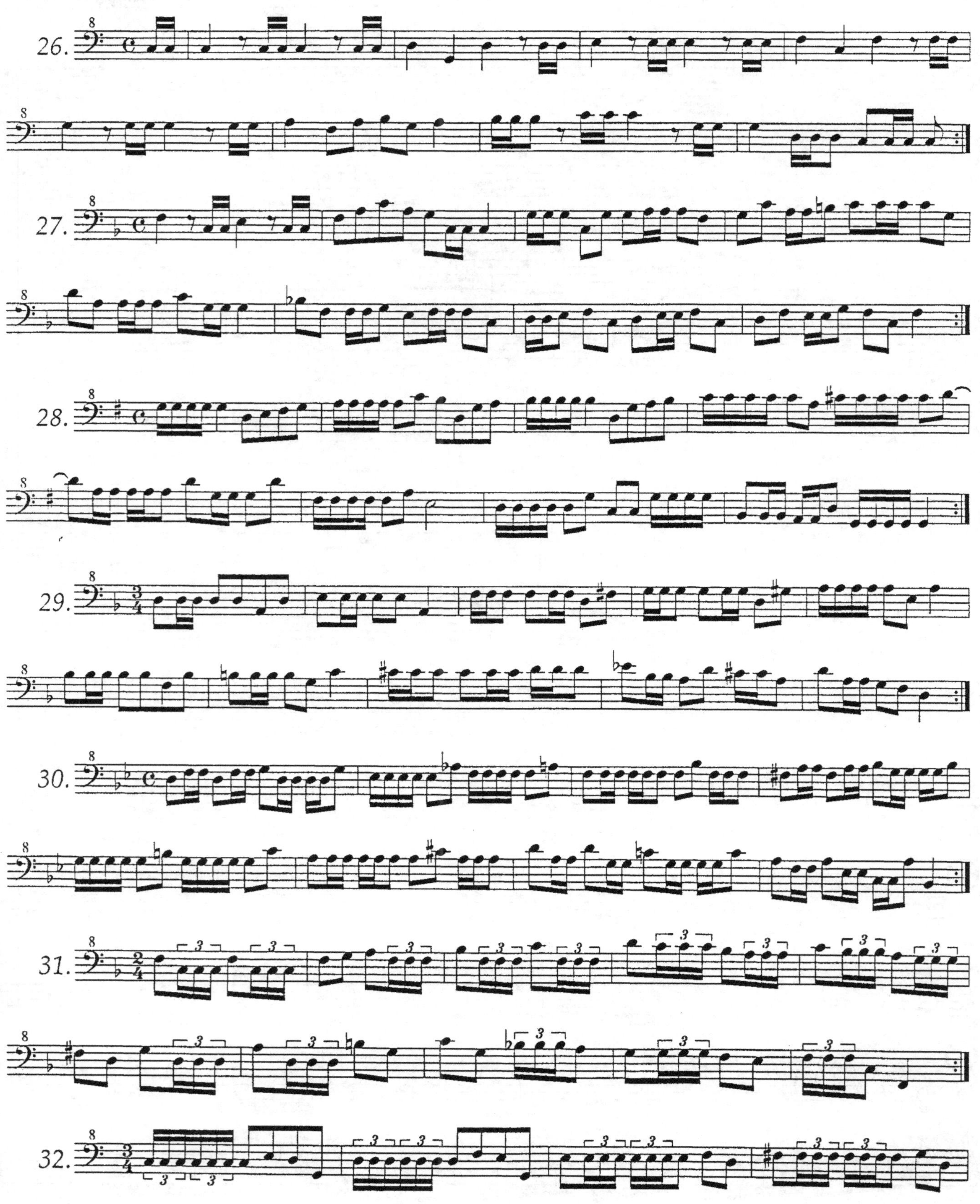

33.
34.
35.
36.
37.
38.

# The Recorder Consort

A consort of recorders consisting of soprano, alto, tenor, and bass can be a most pleasing sound (if played in tune) but it must be remembered that these instruments to not correspond to their vocal counterparts in the same written registers. The recorder consort actually sounds an octave higher than singers or instruments of the same voice categories. As long as no other linear instruments are not mixed in with recorders, the effect to the ear is of a complete SATB relationship. As soon as other instruments are added to recorders, attention must be paid to proper register relationships. For instance, a bass recorder cannot be used as a bass instrument if other instruments are playing at actual pitch. (It can be used as an alto instrument, however.)

A quartet of singers or instruments sounding at pitch can be coupled at the octave by a quartet of recorders, giving much the same effect as a coupling of eight- and four-foot stops on organ or harpsichord.

Let us look at a typical SATB part song of the renaissance and see what the instrumental possibilities are:

*Now, O Now I Needs Must Part*

John Dowland (1563-1626)

The written ranges of this ayre are:

In order to play this Dowland piece at written pitch using recorders, the soprano part could be played by either a tenor or a bass recorder; the alto part by either a bass or great-bass recorder; the tenor part by a bass recorder (with a low F-sharp key) or a great-bass reecorder; and the bass part could only be played on a contra-bass recorder, which is a rather rare instrument. A tenor or bass gamba, a bass krummhorn, or a rackett could also play the bass part at pitch, any of which, along with the other low recorders would produce a soft, pleasing result. these instrumentations would result in an eight-foot pitch. Notice that the tenor part is written with a small 8 under it. This means that the actual sound is an octave lower as when a tenor voice is singing.

If the piece is to played by a recorder quartet sounding an octave higher (at four-foot pitch) the soprano will read the part as written which automatically will make it 8va., the alto will have to read up an octave, the tenor will read it as written (ignoring the small 8), and the bass reading the part will sound an octave higher.

## *Clefs*

Most, but not all, modern editions of early music replace the original clefs with bass and treble clefs rather than the several movable clefs that composers actually employed. An instrumentalist who wishes to become truly proficient in early music must develop some skill in playing in clefs rather other than the standard two. Even the F and G clef were used as movable clefs and, of course, the C clef could be placed on any line of the staff.

First let's see what the placements of the C clef and their names are:

All of the above placements show where middle C lies on the staff. In addition to these middle C indications there are several 20th-century clef usages that indicate the location of middle C an octave higher. The small 8 under a treble clef sign was developed by some publishing houses to show this placement which is the preference of most (but not all) choral composers today.

The following shows several ways that the octave middle C has been indicated in the 20th century:

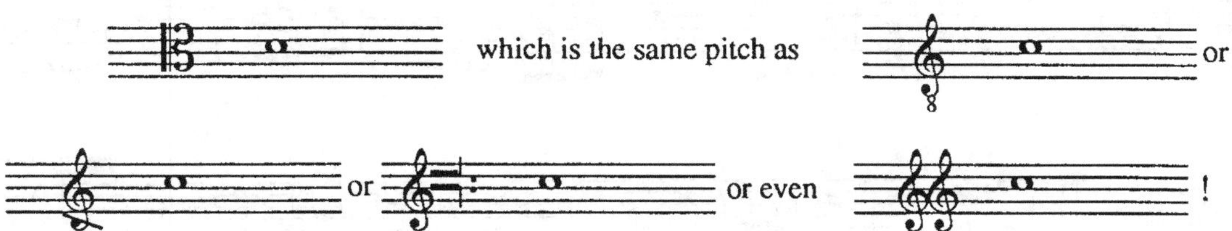


Even the G-clef sign could be used in two different positions:

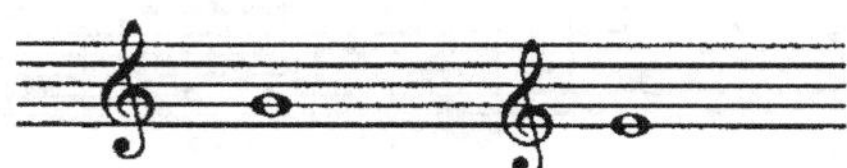

The first of these is the familiar treble clef with the G above middle C on the second line. The second of these placements is called the "French Violin" clef placing the G above middle C on the bottom line. Do not confuse this with the bass clef in which the bottom-line G is two octaves lower. J. S. Bach used this clef for recorders in several of his cantatas.

There are three positions of the F clef, the placement of which shows where the F below middle C is:

The first of these is another form of the baritone clef that is exactly the same as the C clef sign placed on the top line. The second is our standard bass clef and the third is simply a low position of the bass clef. (The term "contra-bass" is actually a misnomer.

In reading clefs other than the standard treble and bass, the proper octave has to be determined. As recorders are at four-foot pitch this will mean an octave higher than indicated. (A small "8" over each clef sign will have to be understood.) If one or more recorders are used with other linear instruments sounding at pitch, the choice of the proper instrument, capable of playing at the indicated pitch, must be made.

The following exercises are to provide some experience in the reading of these obsolete clefs. The author has fudged a bit and given you the fingerings for the starting notes:

Soprano Recorder (sounding 8va) first note fingered:
Soprano Clef

1.

Soprano Recorder (8va) first note fingered:
Mezzo-Soprano Clef

2.

Alto Recorder (8va) first note fingered:
Soprano Clef

3.

Alto Recorder (8va) first note fingered:
Mezzo-Soprano Clef

4.

Alto Recorder (8va) first note fingered:
Alto Clef
5.
Tenor Recorder (8va) first note fingered:
Alto Clef
6.
Tenor Recorder (8va) first note fingered:
Tenor Clef
7.
Tenor Recorder (8va) first note fingered:
Bass Clef
8.
Tenor Recorder (8va) first note fingered:
Baritone Clef (both forms)
9.
Bass Recorder (8va) first note fingered:
Tenor Clef
10.

# *Concerto from Cantata No. 142*

This is Bach's original notation for two alto recorders in the French-violin clef.

J. S. Bach

In the following studies the student will have to determine which member or members of the recorder family to use in order to play each piece either at pitch or an octave higher. The first thing to do is to look at the range of each piece in order to choose the best instrument to fit that range. Some of the pieces can only be played an octave higher while some of them can be played where notated as well as at the octave depending on which instrument is chosen.

## *Duetto from Cantata No. 42*

J. S. Bach

18.

tr

# Characteristic Etudes

1. E-natural

2. B-flat

3. B-natural

4. A-natural

5. C-natural

1. E-natural
2. D-natural
3. E-flat
4. G-flat

1. B-flat
2. B-natural
3. C-sharp, D-flat
4. E-natural

Bass Recorder

*Allegro*

4.

*rit.*

F
5.
Allegretto
(8)
rit.

(8)
Allegro
6.

Bass Recorder
7.
a tempo
poco rit.
rall.

Nore: If played on an alto recorder, this study must be read up an octave; if played on sopranino it will sound up two octaves (two octaves is a fifteenth).

C
9.
rit.

F
10.
(8)
rit.

Bass Recorder
11.
rit.

12.
rit.

F
13.
(8)
rit.

Bass Recorder
14.

©
15.
(8)
rit.

F
16.

Bass Recorder
17.
rit.

©
18.
(8)

F
19.
(8)
7
7

Bass Recorder
20.
8
rit.

©
21.
(8)
rit.

F
22.
(8)
(8)
(8)
(8)
(8)
(8)
(8)
(8)
(8)
(8)
(8)

# *Duos for Various Combinations of Recorders*

## *1. Rondino*

for Soprano and Alto or Tenor and Bass (8va bassa) Recorders

Andrew Charlton

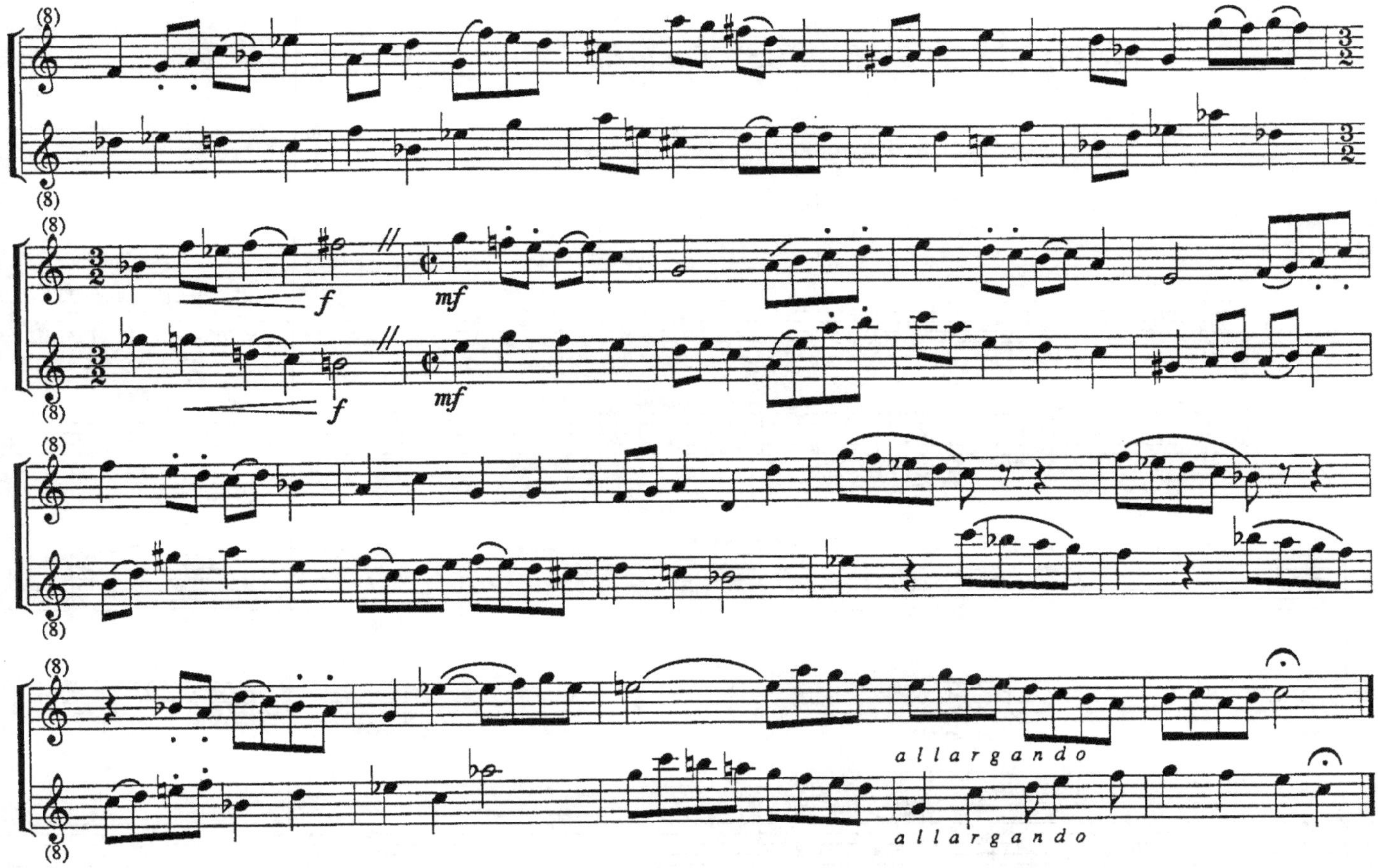

f
mf
f
mf
allargando
allargando

## 2. *Canon at the Fifth*

Andrew Charlton

For Soprano and Alto Recorders

The soprano starts first at the beginning. When the soprano gets to the asterisk, the alto starts at the beginning using C-recorder fingerings. This will mean that the alto will sound a fifth below the soprano as if reading in the mezzo-soprano clef.

Sop.
Alto
*
alto
sop.

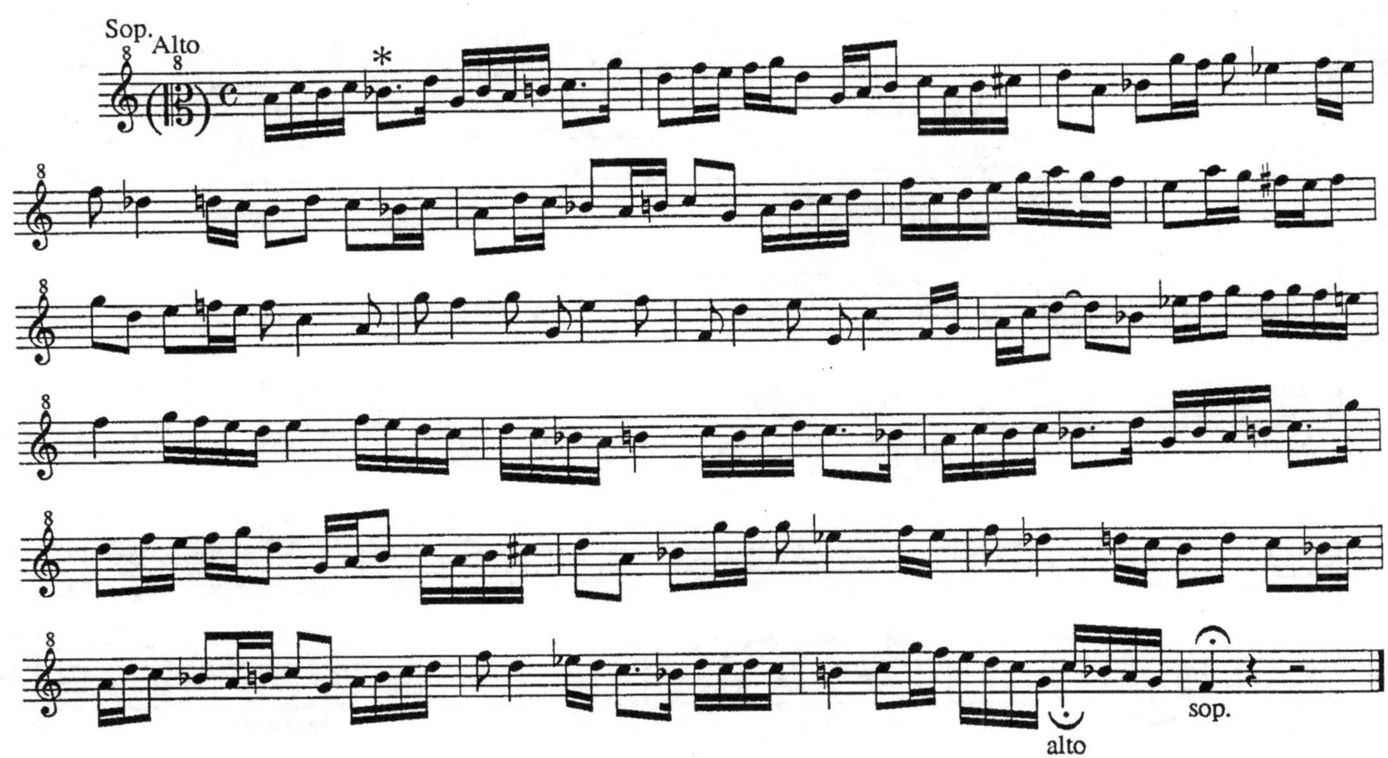

# 3. *Fantasie*

Giovanni Coperario (c. 1575-1626)

For Soprano (or Alto 8va) and Tenor Recorders

tr

# 4. *La Bandoline*

François Couperin (1668-1773)

For Alto and Bass Recorders

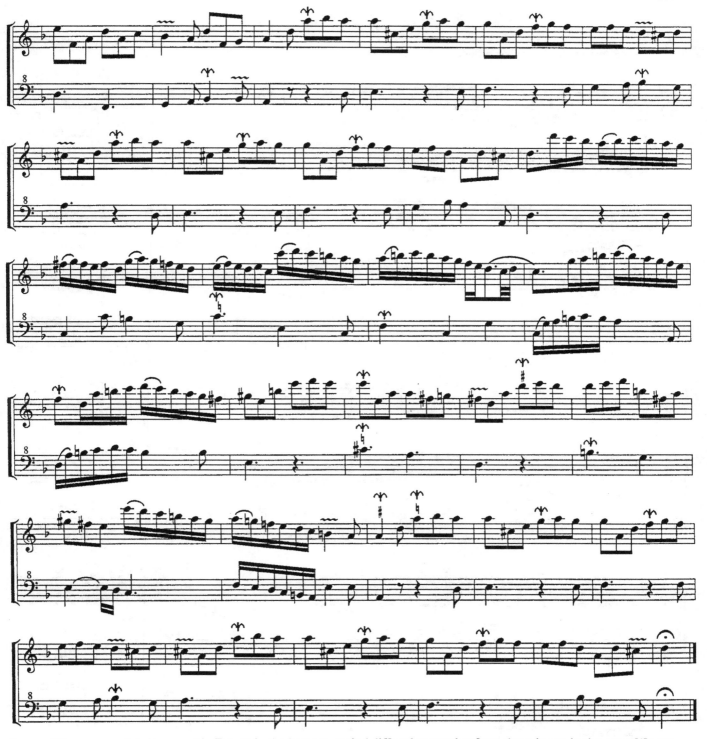

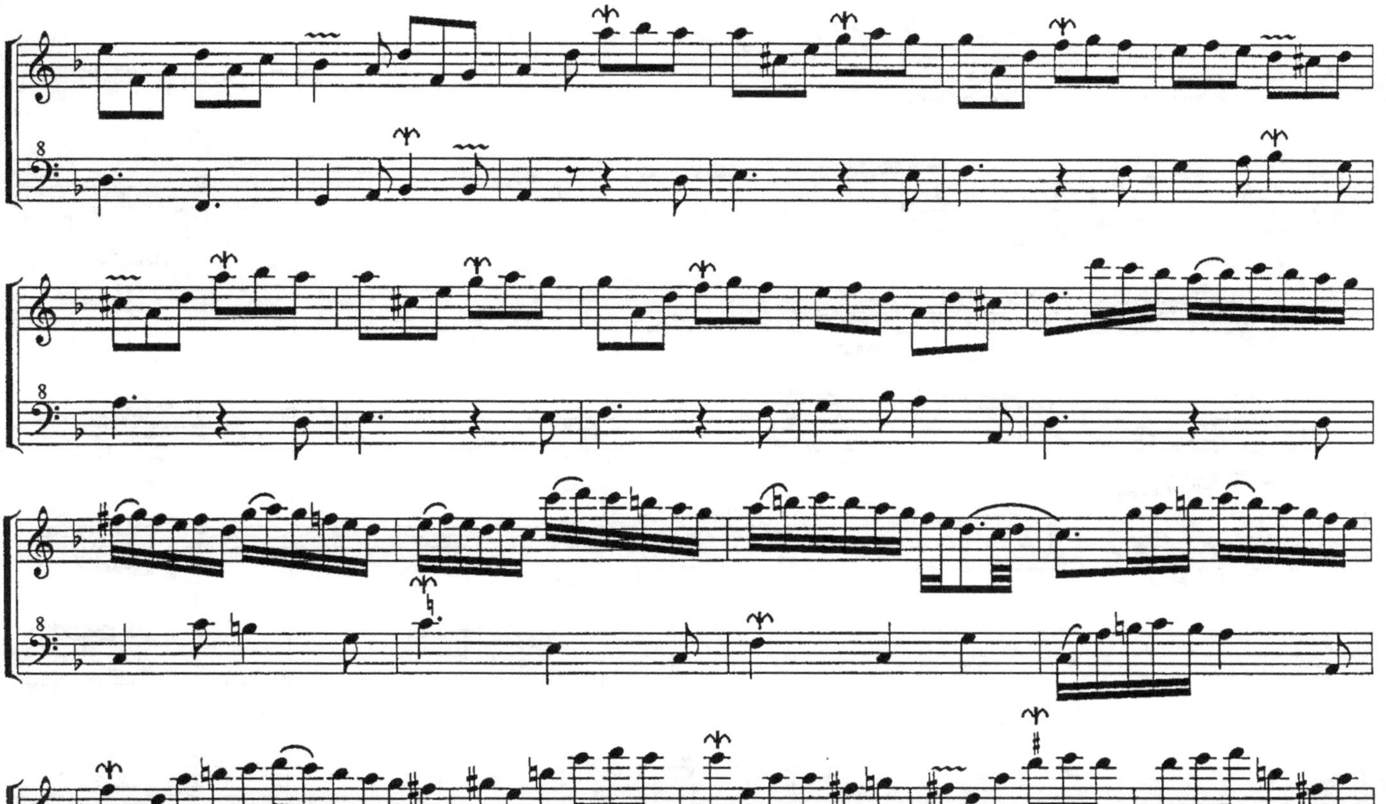

Some of the ornamental signs used in France in the baroque period differed somewhat from those in use in the rest of Europe.

The sign 𝆗 is the mordent and ~~~ is the pralltriller

The mordent

Short trill (pralltriller)

Short trill approached by step

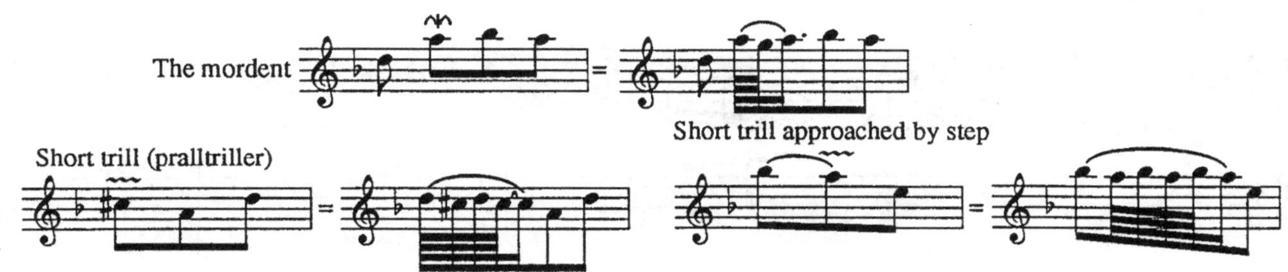

## 5. *Allegro from Suite No. 10*

G. F. Handel (1685-1759)

For Soprano and Tenor Recorders

# 6. Sonata

Maurizio Cazzata (c. 1620-1677)

For Alto (8va.) and Tenor Recorders

Presto
tr
tr
Prestissimo

tr

# 7. *Bicinium*

Erhard Bodenschatz (1575-1636)

For Alto and Tenor Recorders

# 8. Canzonet

Thomas Morley (c. 1557-c. 1603)

For Two Soprano or Two Tenor Recorders

# 9. *Passamezzo Moderne*

For Alto (or Sopranino) Recorder and Guitar

Diego Ortiz (c. 1525-?)

## *10. Canon at the Unison*

Andrew Charlton

For two Soprano or Tenor Recorders

The second player starts at the beginning
when the first player arrives at the asterisk.

# *11. Fugue*

John Blow (1648-1706)

For Soprano and Alto Recorders

# *12. Bicinium*

Antoine Brumel (15th-16th Centuries)

Alto and Tenor (or Two Tenor) Recorders

A. (T.)

T.

# *13. Ductia*

Anon. (c. 13th Century)

For Tenor and Bass Recorders

T.

B.

## 14. Vivace

G. P. Telemann (1681-1767)

For Soprano and Alto Recorders (or Tenor and Bass 8va bassa)

# *15. Blues for Two*

For Soprano and Bass Recorders

Andrew Charlton

CPSIA information can be obtained
at www.ICGtesting.com
Printed in the USA
BVHW010825080620
581025BV00006B/181